GLOBAL AGENDA
FOR SOCIA

VOLU

Edited by
Glenn W. Muschert, Kristen M. Budd,
Michelle Christian, Brian V. Klocke,
Jon Shefner, and Robert Perrucci

First published in Great Britain in 2018 by

Policy Press
University of Bristol
1-9 Old Park Hill
Bristol
BS2 8BB
UK
t: +44 (0)117 954 5940
pp-info@bristol.ac.uk
www.policypress.co.uk

North America office:
Policy Press
c/o The University of Chicago Press
1427 East 60th Street
Chicago, IL 60637, USA
t: +1 773 702 7700
f: +1 773-702-9756
sales@press.uchicago.edu
www.press.uchicago.edu

British Library Cataloguing in Publication Data
A catalogue record for this book is available from the British Library

Library of Congress Cataloging-in-Publication Data
A catalog record for this book has been requested

ISBN 978-1-4473-4912-9 paperback
ISBN 978-1-4473-5220-4 ePdf
ISBN 978-1-4473-4913-6 ePub
ISBN 978-1-4473-4914-3 Mobi

Cover design by Policy Press
Front cover image: iStock

Table of Contents

President's Welcome

Luis A. Fernandez

Historians will look back at the ongoing year as a global turning point. The world is changing, and not all of the changes are good, healthy, or just. Right-wing movements in Europe are on the rise, the earth is warming at an alarming rate, and global economic inequality is increasing. Further, there is a relentless assault on core values, including democracy, freedom, and equality. In this context, *Global Agenda for Social Justice* is an attempt to address these issues and look for practical solutions that lead us toward a more democratic, free, and equitable world. As the President of the Society for the Study of Social Problems (SSSP), it is my honor to present some of the best scholars in our organization as they address some critical social problems of our time. As you may know, SSSP is an organization committed to scholar activist in the pursuit of social justice. It serves not only as a place of respite, but also a gathering space for those seeking to change the current situation. I am proud to be part of an organization that produces such a fine publication. Thank you to all the contributing authors and to the editorial committee, including Glenn W. Muschert, Kristen M. Budd, Michelle Christian, Brian V. Klocke, Jon Shefner, and Robert Perrucci. May your collective work reach the ears of the powerful.

Editorial Introduction

Glenn W. Muschert and Kristen M. Budd

Philosophers have hitherto only interpreted the world in various ways; the point is to change it.

Karl Marx, Eleventh Thesis on Feuerbach

It is an honor to write this editorial introduction on May 5, 2018, the 200th birthday of one of the founders of modern sociology, Karl Marx. Inscribed on Marx's grave marker, his Eleventh Thesis on Feuerbach remains particularly apt as a point of departure for this volume. Indeed, the quote expresses the positive value of the engaged intellect coupled with the inspiration to share academic knowledge to empower those challenging oppression, giving voice to social rights, and resisting exploitation.

Like our forerunner Marx, we the editors of this volume are engaged not only in the academic pursuit of sociological knowledge, but also in the pursuit of social justice in the real world. Nearly all social scientists have studied Marx's ideas as a rite of passage in graduate studies; however, it seems that Marxist sociology is not currently among the dominant paradigms in western social sciences. Nonetheless, many critical and progressive scholars in a variety of social science fields continue to value Marx for his scholarship, and in particular for the sentiment expressed in the Eleventh Thesis on Feuerbach.

Marx reminds us that ideas and knowledge are rather impotent unless they are practically applied to improve the material conditions of social life. Thus, we practice a type of sociology which seeks to broaden discourse beyond the ivory tower, and to disseminate sociological knowledge as accessibly and widely as possible, with the intention that such efforts will increase the likelihood that reliable knowledge will be applied in the world of policy.

This project traces its inspiration back the Presidential Address delivered in 2000 at the annual meetings of the Society for the Study of Social Problems (SSSP), in which Professor Robert Perrucci called upon the Society to redouble its efforts to engage in publicly relevant social science. Dr. Perrucci's speech took place at the 50th Annual Meeting of the SSSP, marking the end of the first half-century of the

SSSP, and setting its agenda as it moved into the 21st century. To put this new agenda into action, a new committee was formed, the Justice 21 Committee, whose mission is to undertake the challenge set by Dr. Perrucci to contribute to a public sociology of social problems, calling for a "report to the nation" to be produced by the SSSP every four years, corresponding with major U.S. Presidential and Congressional elections. In this report, social scientific knowledge about pressing social problems were to be presented in jargon-free language, which in comparison to many academic publications, would be widely accessible. Dr. Perrucci's vision was to make the best available research about social problems accessible not only to politicians, journalists, and policy makers, but also to the public. The Justice 21 Committee operates under the broader authority of the SSSP, and specifically pursues one goal of the SSSP, which is "to encourage problem-centered social research and to foster cooperative relations among persons and organizations engaged in the application of scientific sociological findings to the formulation of social policies." The publication of the *Agenda for Social Justice* has been this committee's major effort in advancing the public sociology of social problems.

The first of these volumes was self-published by the Justice 21 Committee as a pamphlet in 2004, and from those modest origins, this project began to develop. In subsequent iterations, namely 2008 and 2012, the volume became increasingly professional in its appearance and prominence. Beginning in 2016, the *Agenda for Social Justice* was published by an academic publisher, Policy Press, whose values align closely with the SSSP. Policy Press prides itself as a scholarly publishing house (affiliated with the University of Bristol, UK and with distribution via the University of Chicago Press), whose role is to advance "the use of research evidence to improve policy making, practice, or social well-being." All past volumes are available via open access at the following link: https://www.sssp1.org/index.cfm/m/323/locationSectionId/0/Agenda_for_Social_Justice.

Until now, the *Agenda for Social Justice* has focused exclusively on U.S.-based problems, research, and solutions. However, as Policy Press is a publisher with international reach, we decided to launch another volume focusing on global and international social problems, which is scheduled to appear at four-year intervals beginning in 2018. The volume you hold in your hands is the first iteration of this global edition, which is entitled *Global Agenda for Social Justice*. The volume contains 16 topical chapters followed by a 17th chapter and an Afterword, which examine the nature of global social problems more generally. Each of the 16 substantive chapters concentrates on a social problem which is global or international in scope. As always, each chapter follows the specific three-part format of: 1) defining the social problem; 2) summarizing research evidence about the problem; and 3) presenting concrete and practical policy interventions/responses which are likely to mitigate, reduce, or abolish the problem.

The volume has six sections, each of which contains chapters examining related issues and themes. Section 1 focuses on Policing and Criminal (In)Justice, with chapters on the war on drugs, police discrimination, wrongful convictions, and the criminalization of HIV status. Section 2 focuses on Environmental Issues, with chapters on exposure to radiation, natural disasters, and energy policy. Section 3 focuses on Gender and Sexuality, with chapters on masculinities and sex education. Section 4 focuses on Violence against Precarious Groups, with chapters on violence against migrants, violence against sex workers, genocide, and torture. Section 5 focuses on Inequalities and Disparities, with chapters on food insecurity, pensions for informal sector workers, and digital exclusion. Finally, Section 6 offers a Look Forward, with chapters focusing on global social problems more generally, including an afterword to provide a closing perspective.

The list of contributors for this volume is an impressive and diverse group of social scientists from a variety of nations, including researchers, policy analysts, and activists at all levels of academic participation including graduate students, NGO researchers, and assistant, associate, full, and emeritus professors. The brief biographies listed at the end of the volume reveal that the current assemblage of scholars represented in this volume are quite prestigious, having extensive scholarly, teaching, and practical/applied experience. Unfortunately, space does not allow the inclusion of the numerous research articles and books by our contributors, but suffice it to say that many are extremely prolific.

It is worth mentioning that the *Global Agenda for Social Justice* is not conceived as all-inclusive coverage of all pressing social problems. The editors put out a worldwide call for proposals, and received an overwhelming response (over 85 proposals from six continents). It was our difficult task to cull this list of potential chapters to the 17 included in the volume, yet we could only select from the pool of proposals received. We note that certain pressing global problems are not represented here; for example, climate change, excessive militarism/ endless war, global inequality, risk of nuclear war or disaster, and terrorism. Nonetheless, the issues included are wide-ranging and certainly are among the pressing social justice issues facing the world today.

It is the Justice 21 Committee's hope that this volume will be influential in public and policy discourse, both for its individual chapters and as a whole. If students, the general public, policy makers, and scholars are better informed of the nature of these pressing problems and their solutions, then we will have achieved our goal. Please take the enclosed pieces highlighting research and policy solutions into classrooms, community discussions, discussions with peers, and indeed into the broader public discourse. In that you will be cooperating in our effort to inspire helpful action for reducing or eliminating the world's social problems, as we work to create a more inclusive, equitable, democratic, and just world. That is, in keeping with Marx's Eleventh Thesis on Feuerbach, it is our hope that this volume will not only be useful in creating greater understanding of social problems, but also that these ideas will have utility in creating real-world solutions to those problems.

Acknowledgements

Though relatively concise, producing this volume would nonetheless have been impossible without the cooperation and support of many good people. We the editors would like to thank our authors first, for working with us and for their quality contributions. It is a pleasure to work with such a group of professionals to bring these ideas to print. As always, we are indebted to Michele Koontz and Héctor Delgado of the SSSP administrative and executive offices, respectively, for their support and encouragement. We thank acquisitions editor Victoria Pittman and her team at Policy Press, with whom we are pleased to collaborate on this book. We thank all the students, scholars, and activists who make the SSSP such an exciting environment in which to study, research, write, and undertake meaningful social action.

Finally, this volume is dedicated to the memory of Professor JoAnn Miller, a founding member of the Justice 21 Committee, who passed away much too soon.

About the Society for the Study of Social Problems

The Society for the Study of Social Problems (the SSSP), is an academic and action-oriented professional association, whose purpose is to promote and protect social science research and teaching about significant social problems in society. Members of the SSSP include students, faculty members at educational institutions, researchers, practitioners, and advocates.

Some of the SSSP's core activities include encouraging rigorous research, nurturing young sociologists, focusing on solutions to the problems of society, fostering cooperative relations between the academic and the policy and/or social action spheres.

If you would like to learn more about joining the SSSP, reading our publications, or attending our annual conference, please visit the SSSP website: www.sssp1.org.

Finally, please consider supporting the SSSP, a nonprofit 501(c) 3 organization which accepts tax deductible contributions both in support of its general operations and for specific purposes. It is possible to donate to the SSSP in general, but it is also possible to donate in support of specific efforts. If you would like to encourage the kind of public sociology represented in this book, please consider supporting the efforts of the Justice 21 Committee. For information on contributing, please visit www.sssp1.org/index.cfm/m/584/.

Notes on Contributors

Ajanaw Alemie, MSW, received his M.S.W. degree from Addis Ababa University, Ethiopia. He served as the Head of the Department of Social Work at Gondar University, Ethiopia, and is currently a Lecturer there. He was a visiting scholar to Dominican University in 2017, where he worked on revising the social work program at the University of Gondar. His research interests are in issues surrounding the elderly in Ethiopia. He has presented at international conferences and is interested in international social work and how principles of social work practice in various nations can be applied to the Ethiopian context.

Robert Aponte, Ph.D., is an Associate Professor of Sociology at IUPUI with specializations in the Drug Issues, Latino Studies and Urban Poverty.

Kyle C. Ashlee, MS, Colorado State University, is a doctoral candidate in the Student Affairs in Higher Education Program at Miami University. Kyle's scholarly interests include critical perspectives on race and gender in higher education. He has authored many peer-reviewed articles, chapters, and an award-winning book. Kyle has developed educational programs around the world, including a masculinities theater group in Switzerland, an Intergroup Dialogue program at Yale National University Singapore, and Miami University's first-ever academic course on masculinities. He was awarded the *2016 Social Justice Educator of the Year,* and the *2018 Harry Canon Outstanding Professional* with ACPA College Educators International.

Rosemary Barberet is Professor in the Sociology Department at John Jay College of Criminal Justice. Her research interests include the use of criminal justice data and research in policy making, victimization, and gender. Fluent in Spanish and French, she has chaired the International Division of the American Society of Criminology (ASC). She has received the Herbert Bloch Award of the ASC, the Rafael Salillas Award of the Sociedad Espanola de Investigación Criminológica, and the Sarah Hall and Linda Saltzman Awards from the Division on Women and Crime of the ASC. She is the author of the award-winning book, *Women, Crime and Criminal Justice: A Global Enquiry.* Dr. Barberet represents the International Sociological Association (ISA) at the United Nations.

Edwin Bernard is the Global Coordinator of the HIV Justice Network, which works with organizations around the world who want to see the end of criminal or similar laws, policies, and practices that regulate, control, and punish people living with HIV based on their HIV-positive status. Edwin also coordinates the HIV Justice Worldwide campaign, a coalition of ten civil society organizations that are working together to end HIV criminalization. Edwin has been contributing to global knowledge of, and advocacy against, HIV criminalization since he wrote his first book on the subject in 2007.

Tirth Bhatta is an Assistant Professor in the department of sociology at University of Nevada Las Vegas. His primary area of research focuses on the contributing role of structural forces in producing heterogeneity or disparities in later-life health outcomes. His research seeks to understand how cumulative life-course socioeconomic status intersects with other forms of stratification (especially race and gender) to shape later-life health disparities in the U.S. and internationally. His work has appeared in various journals including *Journal of Gerontology: Social Sciences* and *Journal of Aging and Health*.

Craig Boylstein is an associate professor of Sociology at Coastal Carolina University. His research interests include the lived experience of chronic illness, the impact of local, state, and federal drug laws, and police use-of-force. His most recent work is *When Police Use Force: Context, Methods, Outcomes* (Lynne Rienner Publishers, 2018).

Kristen M. Budd is an assistant professor of sociology and criminology at Miami University. Her research focuses on sexually motivated interpersonal violence, including social and legal responses to interpersonal violence.

Brandon Cash, BM, BA, St. Olaf College, is a graduate student in the Student Affairs in Higher Education Master's program and residence life professional at Miami University. His interests consist primarily of masculinity and sexual and interpersonal violence prevention and response within the context of institutions of higher education.

Michelle Christian is an Assistant Professor in the Department of Sociology at the University of Tennessee-Knoxville. Her research focuses on structural racism, global political economy and precarious forms of labour.

Jacqueline Daugherty, PhD, is an interdisciplinary sociologist that works at the intersection of sexuality, inequality, education, and political economy. She is a Lecturer in the Western Program for Individualized Studies at Miami University, and is a member of SSSP. She has also worked in the nonprofit sector for over a decade as a school and community-based sexuality educator, and has seen at first hand the consequences of poor sexuality education. Jacqueline understands access to comprehensive sexuality education is a human right and a requirement for building a more equitable and peaceful society and world.

Carrie Foote is an Associate Professor of Sociology at IUPUI where she teaches courses on the sociology of health and illness, particularly HIV/AIDS, and qualitative methods. Her current scholarship focuses on HIV criminalization experiences and reform efforts. She has been living with HIV for over 30 years, served on numerous HIV clinical, care, and prevention advisory boards, is a founding member of the Prevention Access Undetectable=Untransmittable Campaign, and chairs the HIV Modernization Movement Indiana – an effort to modernize Indiana's HIV criminal laws.

Richelle Frabotta, MSEd, CSE, CSES, a community-based Sexuality Educator since 1992, is a Certified Sexuality Educator by the American Association of Sexuality Educators, Counselors and Therapists since 1996 and Supervisor since 2014. She occupies Miami University (Oxford, Ohio), where she serves as Instructor in the Family Science and Social Work Department, is Coordinator of Sexuality Education and birthing the Dennis L. Carlson Sexuality Education Studies Center, while completing her doctoral program in Leadership, Culture and Curriculum. Richelle has a profound respect for diversity, believes in prevention education, endeavoring to empower people to make healthy choices for sexual pleasure and wellness.

Shannon Golden is a Research Associate with the Center for Victims of Torture (CVT), a human rights organization working to end the practice of torture and provide rehabilitation for survivors since 1985. She completed her PhD in sociology and human rights at the University of Minnesota. She studies how individuals and communities reconstruct their lives after widespread violence and gross human rights violations. Her co-authored book, *Taking Root: Human Rights and Public Opinion in the Global South*, analyzes public views on human rights ideas and issues, including the use of torture.

Hannah Hurrle is undergraduate double major in Sociology and Philosophy at IUPUI.

Vasundhara Kaul is a graduate student in the Sociology Department at Purdue University. Her main research interests are in the areas of gender (and its intersections with caste and class), development, and water and environmental justice. She currently works on a collaborative project about women in sex work and violence. Vasundhara has over four years of experience in conducting impact and program evaluations across multiple thematic areas, such as gender and education and issues of water and sanitation in India.

Brian V. Klocke, PhD is a Visiting Associate Professor at Washington College. His collaborative and singular research on social movements, moral panic, masculinities, and media framing has appeared in the peer-reviewed journals of *Sociology Compass*, *Policing and Society*, *Men and Masculinities*, *Journalism Studies*, *Journalism*, and in the books, *Lost in Media: The Ethics of Everyday Life*, and *The Ashgate Research Companion to Moral Panics*. He is co-author of *The Better World Handbook: From Good Intentions to Everyday Actions* and has a chapter in *Sociologists in Action on Inequalities: Race, Class, Gender, and Sexuality*. He is also a member of the leadership team of Faculty Against Rape (http://www. facultyagainstrape.net).

Nirmala Lekhak is an Assistant Professor in the School of Nursing at University of Nevada Las Vegas. Her research investigates the effectiveness of non-pharmacological interventions (e.g. meditation) in promoting psychological wellbeing of dementia caregivers and in preventing or mitigating the cognitive decline in later life associated with multimorbidity and socioeconomic disadvantage. Her work has appeared in various journals including *Western Journal of Nursing Research* and *Journal of Gerontology: Social Sciences*.

Michael Loeffelman, MEd, University of Virginia, is a Ph.D. student in Curriculum Studies at Purdue University. His research focuses on the intersection of higher education, masculinity, community engagement, and public pedagogy. Mike has worked with college students for the past 12 years. Specifically, he has worked with students in residence life, judicial affairs, community engagement, honors, and academic advising. He has worked with male college students in a variety of different capacities. Currently, Mike is an academic advisor at Miami

University and has worked previously at the Rhode Island School of Design, East Carolina University, and Purdue University.

Terance D. Miethe is a professor of Criminal Justice at the University of Nevada, Las Vegas. He is the author of several books and articles on the death penalty, criminal punishments, and other types of state-sponsored social control.

Miranda Mirosa is a Senior Lecturer in the Department of Food Science, University of Otago. With a background in marketing and consumer behavior, her interdisciplinary research seeks to understand why people eat what they do, why they don't eat what they don't, and how people can be supported to eat quality, healthy and environmentally sustainable foods. Her current research focus is food waste, with work including establishing the University of Otago Food Waste Innovation Research Group, collaborating with colleagues on research in China and Australia, and contributing to the APEC project Strengthening Public-Private Partnership to Reduce Food Losses, and the National Consumer Food Waste Reduction project run by the New Zealand waste industry body WASTEMinz.

Glenn W. Muschert, PhD, University of Colorado, is Professor in the Sociology, Criminology, and Social Justice Studies Programs at Miami University. His scholarly interests lie in the sociological study of social problems, including the mass media discourse of school shootings, moral panics, and electronic surveillance technologies. He has published various articles and chapters in the fields of sociology, criminology, and media studies. His recent books include *School Shootings: Mediatized Violence in a Global Age*; *The Digital Divide: The Internet and Social Inequality in International Perspective*; *Responding to School Violence: Confronting the Columbine Effect*; and *Theorizing Digital Divides*.

Eric Mykhalovskiy is a Professor of Sociology at York University in Toronto. Over the past ten years he has published widely on the topic of HIV criminalization. In 2017, he received the Canadian Association for HIV Research/Canadian Foundation for AIDS Research Excellence in Research Award for the Social Sciences. Eric is a senior editor of the *Canadian Journal of Public Health*, a founding member of the Ontario Working Group on Criminal Law and HIV Exposure, and a board member of the Canadian HIV/AIDS Legal Network.

Majia H. Nadesan is Professor of Communication Studies at Arizona State University where she studies and teaches the (bio)politics of risk. Her most recent books include *Crisis Communications, Liberal Democracy and Ecological Sustainability* (2016) and *Fukushima and the Privatization of Risk* (2013).

Zachary D. Palmer is a PhD candidate in the Sociology Department at Purdue University. His research area is social inequality with a focus on gender (and its intersections with race and class) and masculinities. His current projects examine the politics of men's rights movements in the United States and India, gender in the academy, and the experiences of sex workers and transgender people in India. His research has been published in *Sociological Focus* and he has presented at sociological conferences within and outside the U.S.

Robert Perrucci is professor of sociology emeritus at Purdue University. His 19 books and 90 articles and chapters focus on organizations and structures of inequality.

Massimo Ragnedda, PhD is a Senior Lecturer in Mass Communication at Northumbria University, Newcastle, UK, where he conducts research on the digital divide and social media. He has authored or edited ten books, including *Theorizing the Digital Divides*, co-edited with Glenn Muschert (2017); *The third Digital Divide: A Weberian Approach to Digital Inequalities* (2017); and *The Digital Divide: The Internet and Social Inequality in International Perspective*, co-edited with Glenn Muschert (2013). His scholarship has also appeared in numerous peer-reviewed journals, and book chapters in English, Spanish, Italian, and Portuguese texts.

David Reynolds graduated from the University of Otago with a MA in Sociology in 2016. He has worked on a range of food-related projects with researchers at the University of Otago in the Centre for Sustainability, the Department of Sociology, Gender and Social Work, and the Department of Food Science. Before commencing a Ph.D. at Monash University, he is publishing material drawing on his Master's thesis, "The Depoliticisation of Deprivation: Food Insecurity in Aotearoa New Zealand." He is interested in the politics and material practicalities involved in people eating as they do, with a focus the themes of social justice, environmental impact and sustainability.

Diana Rodriguez-Spahia is a PhD candidate in the Criminal Justice Doctoral Program at John Jay College of Criminal Justice/ The Graduate Center of the City University of New York, with a specialization in Policy, Oversight and Administration. She has taught courses in criminal justice and sociology at John Jay College of Criminal Justice and Rutgers University. Her research interests include international criminal justice, terrorism, the crime–gender nexus, media, human rights and policy making. She was the managing editor of the journal, *Feminist Criminology* for four years. She is a recipient of numerous research and teaching awards, including the Teaching Excellent Award from the Sociology Department at John Jay College of Criminal Justice and the inaugural Graduate Center Award for Excellence in Teaching.

Moushumi Roy earned her PhD in Sociology from Michigan State University. She is the editor of *Construction of Social Problems: An Anthology*. Dr. Roy's research examines how social processes and determinants including individual and collective mode of interactions determine self-assessed health outcomes among immigrants of Asian ancestry in the U.S. While broader focus is on the population of Asian ancestry, she also investigates self-assessed health outcomes among paramedics (health care workers) of Asian Indian origin.

Joachim J. Savelsberg, Dr. rer. pol. is Professor of Sociology and Law and Arsham and Charlotte Ohanessian Chair, University of Minnesota. He was educated in his native Germany. Visiting professor or fellow at Harvard University, Johns Hopkins University, Ludwig-Maximilians-Universität München, Karl Franzens Universität Graz, Humboldt Universität Berlin, Rockefeller Bellagio Center, and Käte Hamburger Center for Advanced Study "Law as Culture," Bonn. Past research on comparative criminal punishment, sentencing and the field of criminology. Recent work and publications on human rights issues, especially effects of legal intervention on collective representations and memories of mass atrocities: *Representing Mass Violence: Conflicting Responses to Human Rights Violations in Darfur* (University of California Press, 2015); *American Memories: Atrocities and the Law* (with Ryan D. King; Russell Sage Foundation, 2011); *Crime and Human Rights: Criminology of Genocide and Atrocities* (Sage, 2010). For more information see: http://www.joachimsavelsberg.com or https://cla.umn.edu/about/directory/profile/savel001

James L. Scherrer, PhD, LCSW, is an Associate Professor in Dominican University's School of Social Work. He received his Ph.D. in Social Work from the University of Illinois at Chicago's Jane Addams School of Social Work. He has over 40 years of experience in providing child welfare services to poor and inner city youth. Since 2004 he has been active in International Social Work projects. He is on a team that developed a community-based, family-centered child welfare program model in Ethiopia. In addition, he is researching the impact international social work experiences have on a social worker's practice.

Jon Shefner is professor and head of the Department of Sociology at the University of Tennessee, Knoxville. His research focuses on globalization, political economy, and social justice issues in Latin America and beyond.

Leland G. Spencer, PhD, University of Georgia, 2013, is Associate Professor in the Department of Interdisciplinary and Communication Studies and affiliate faculty in the Department of Media, Journalism, and Film, as well as the Women's, Gender, and Sexuality Studies Program at Miami University. An award-winning scholar, he is author of *Women Bishops and Rhetorics of Shalom* (Lexington, 2017) and co-editor of *Transgender Communication Studies* (Lexington, 2015). Leland has published more than a dozen peer-reviewed scholarly journal articles in outlets such as *Communication Studies*, *Women & Language*, *Queer Studies in Media & Popular Culture*, *Equity and Excellence in Education*, and others.

Mangala Subramaniam is Professor of Sociology and Chair and Director of the Susan Bulkeley Butler Center for Leadership Excellence at Purdue University. Her research addresses social inequality in global contexts – gender, race, caste, and class issues and their intersections – and the dynamics of state and social movements. Her current projects focus on the politics of HIV prevention; environmental justice, specifically water rights; gender and violence; and women's careers in the academy. Her research has been published in *Current Sociology, Gender & Society,* and *Mobilization* among many others. She is the incoming Associate Editor of *Social Problems*. See https://web.ics.purdue.edu/~msubrama

Sean Sweeney, PhD, is the Director of the Joseph S. Murphy Institute's International Program on Labor, Climate, and the Environment at the City University of New York. Sean is also the coordinator of

Trade Unions for Energy Democracy, which is a global network of 42 unions from 16 countries advocating for democratic control and social ownership of energy resources and infrastructure.

Tereza Trejbalová is a third-year PhD student of criminology and criminal justice at University of Nevada, Las Vegas. She obtained her Master's degree in Political Science from University of Nevada, Reno. Her research interests include the death penalty in the U.S., Africa, and Asia, male victimization and trauma, females in corrections, and human rights.

Todd E. Vachon is a Postdoctoral Scholar with the Department of Labor Studies and Employment Relations at Rutgers University's School of Management and Labor Relations and the founding President of the Graduate Employee Union, UAW Local 6950 at the University of Connecticut. Todd is actively involved with the Connecticut Roundtable on Climate and Jobs, serves as a member of the Global Advisory Group for Trade Unions for Energy Democracy, and is a member of the National Steering Committee for the Labor Network for Sustainability's Labor Convergence on Climate Change.

SECTION I

Policing and Criminal (In)Justice

ONE

The Worldwide War on Drugs: Advancing Reforms, Circumventing Resistance

Robert Aponte and Hannah Hurrle, IUPUI

The Problem

The Worldwide War on Drugs has long been shown to be an absolute disaster. Increasingly, countries around the world are clamoring for an end to the deadly, costly, and unwinnable policy calamity. Numerous international blue ribbon committees have come out strongly on the need to dismantle the policies, and major protests assailing the drug war have been held in scores of cities throughout the world. The array of harms wreaked by the criticized policies is mind-numbing. These include human rights violations, seizures and/or destruction of properties, and thousands of deaths per annum. Other drug war ills include the spread of diseases (especially HIV), unparalleled enrichment of violent organized criminal enterprises, discriminatory enforcement, wholesale displacement of villages, mass incarceration, corruption on a vast scale, and the wasting of billions of dollars in anti-drug expenditures.

Among the drug war's dysfunctions are some 160,000 dead in Mexico's drug war between the cartels and the government, within a mere decade (2006–2014). An additional 25,000 have disappeared and a whopping 280,000 have been displaced, typically never to return. Some 13,000 are estimated to have been killed in the Philippines since 2016 (mainly extralegal execution, government supported vigilantism, etc.), though officially, fewer than 4,000 thereby perished. In Malaysia, most drug executions only involve marijuana or hashish, both among the least harmful of all drugs. In Iran, where many are executed, 75% of all executions of recent years have involved drug offenses. State executions for drug crimes overall, sometimes for mere possession, have exceeded 1,000 deaths in some years, excluding China. China's execution numbers are state secrets, but are suspected to exceed all other nations' figures. Almost all of these are considered gross violations of human rights by the UN, despite the organization's pro-war rhetoric.

The drug war has also bred widespread corruption internationally. For instance, the former Wachovia bank was sanctioned for laundering hundreds of millions of dollars in drug money, while British banking behemoth HSBC admitted to laundering billions. More recently (2017) Citibank was fined nearly $100 million for such crimes, while earlier, American Express was similarly sanctioned. Notably, no one was jailed. In one of the most egregious instances of corruption, male DEA agents were discovered utilizing sex workers provided by the cartels. Reportedly, they also received cash and other gifts over a couple of years. Despite this monumental betrayal, the Justice Department could not obtain all the details, and the agents were only mildly sanctioned.

These latter findings raise a critical, secondary problem within the nexus of issues here. Specifically, it is that the US and a handful of other nations may derive benefits from the drug war and are not truly committed to its demise. Thus, even as the international chorus for change continues to grow, key UN components resist liberalization. This resistance is known to reflect the will of influential member states.

Research

Worldwide traffic in illicit drugs is estimated to constitute an enterprise worth more than $350 billion dollars a year. Similar to the effects of prohibition in the US, the criminalization of drugs facilitate sellers' ability to amass fortunes through underground markets, which are then self-regulated with violence. Not surprisingly then, the enormous enforcement efforts at curtailing access and distribution have failed. For example, between 1990 and 2007, the inflation-adjusted prices of the "big three," heroin, cocaine, and cannabis, fell by over 80%, while their purity rose by 60%, 11%, and 161%, respectively. Correspondingly, the number of users aged 15–65 rose from an estimated 185 million to 247 million between 2003 and 2014. Seeming advances, such as the eradication of coca crops in one area, typically unleashes harvests elsewhere –akin to a "whack-a-mole" process. Similarly, putting some dealers out of business typically gives rise to others; failures formally recognized by the D.E.A.

The gargantuan profits earned by the trafficking buy more than bribery and lethal power, but also fund terrorism. In Pakistan, the Taliban amassed $700 million in drug money, while the ISIS branches in Syria and Iraq are believed to also earn large sums from drug trafficking. Punitive drug laws also further the spread of diseases, such as HIV and HCV, by deterring users from seeking help, including health care. Denying safe drug-use paraphernalia, such as sterile needles, forces use of riskier products, thereby enabling acquisition/ transmission of ailments. Notably, while the worldwide HIV infection rate dropped some 35% between 2000 and 2014, it rose by 30% in the Eastern Europe/Central Asia area, mainly due to injection drug use in prohibitionist environments.

These increasingly apparent observations have spurred enormous opposition to the war. Over the last few decades, some 30 nations have decriminalized to varying extents. By the early 2010s, the liberalization crescendo seemed unstoppable, as major international agencies and committees uniformly and repeatedly decried the war's continuance. These include such UN agencies as UNAIDS, the WHO, and their human rights officials, among others.

These groups promulgate the remarkable gains in places that have decriminalized and have been studied. Portugal, by far the most celebrated and studied, decriminalized all drug possession in 2001 and has exhibited massive improvements in all relevant indicators. They experienced a 90% drop in drug-related HIV transmissions and an 85% plunge in fatal overdoses, among other gains. Indeed, their policies attract visiting delegations from throughout the world, who come to study the renowned "Portuguese Model."

After a long history of treaties binding the signatories to the drug war, where the liberalization supporters were continuously overruled by the UN's enforcement arm, UNODC, change appears imminent. Prior to the UN's 2016 meeting on the drug war, members of UNODC leaked a draft of a forthcoming report that included a call for decriminalization. The call was later disavowed and removed from the report after a discussion in a closed door meeting that excluded most member-states' representatives, though the report did soften the pro-war language. Nonetheless, anti-war member nations continue to decriminalize, as did Norway's legislators toward the close of 2017, along with Mexico's legalizing of medicinal marijuana that same year. Indeed, even the US, long the major proponent of the drug war, has witnessed several of its component states legalize recreational use of marijuana in recent years. This clearly undermines the nation's leverage at pushing anti-drug initiatives, both at home and abroad.

Recommendations and Solutions

The international authority binding nations to the drug war is currently based in, and organized by, the UN. It rests on a series of treaties spanning the 20th century and into the present, with periodic meetings where amendments can be considered. UN authority is considered binding to all signatory nations. Ending the worldwide war on drugs, therefore, must proceed in one of two basic directions. The process must either entail adjusting the treaties' provisions to reflect the changed outlook, or it may simply dissolve the agreements altogether. There are a number of reasons to expect that total dissolution of the treaties' basic provisions is not likely to be achieved in the short run. For example, there are nations that wish to continue the status quo, and they tend to be influential. In addition, liberalization adherents understand that dismantling the many mechanisms underlying the drug war will take time for the necessary adjustments to be made. Hence, a different approach may be more fruitful in the effort to fully or partially end the drug war.

Because there is some amount of flexibility in how signatory nations organize their domestic regulatory processes bearing on drug use and distribution, it is possible to also move forward in a piecemeal manner, with the various countries carefully shifting their policies in accord with their own interests and capacities. This has made possible the decriminalization moves of many of the signatory nations that have already gone forward. Simply emphasizing and expanding the flexibility will encourage the increased use of policies to eradicate or minimize harm and criminalization. However, on a broader level, the UN's authority can be utilized in ways that will facilitate the transition to a decriminalized world. Specifically, the UN can and must advance a handful of critical principles that will hasten the dismantling of the vast array of harms the drug war has caused. Though these principles may overlap in practice, they are analytically distinct, conceptually, and the overlap merely underlies their paramount importance in the quest for a more just world.

The principles/solutions that the UN must pursue and promulgate without further delay:

1. **Transparency**. Specifically, the very process in which the organization's rule making takes place needs to be open to all members and not subject to secrecy and limited participation. Relying strictly on open and honest democratic practices in UN rule making must be codified as an operating principle. In the

most recent meeting on drug policies, where the majority of states were looking forward to a decriminalization declaration and a draft of just such a document was leaked, the decriminalization principle was hastily withdrawn in a closed meeting with limited participation by member states.

2. **Science**. The structure of the legal and regulatory policies followed and encouraged by the UN's drug-related endeavors should be based on science, not rhetoric or ideology. The claim that a world without any non-medicinal use of drugs is possible through enforcement policies has long been exposed as a farce. Above all else, that prohibitionist principle has allowed the proliferation of powerful underworld syndicates, on the one hand, and mass incarceration of disadvantaged populations on the other. Reversing direction will undermine those underworld groups while ceasing to victimize users. For example, it is already the case that Mexican Cartels have decreased their marijuana shipments to the US as a result of the legalization of the drug in several states.

3. **Proportionality** (fairness, or the punishment should fit the crime). Another necessary principle that the UN must fervently pursue is proportionality. The farcical spectacle of major international bankers going totally unpunished for laundering hundreds of millions of drug dollars, at the same time that less powerful users are harshly punished, sometimes executed, for low-level drug offenses, must end. Such hypocrisy would never continue if subjected to wide exposure and to fairness in the adjudicatory processes.

4. **Intervention**. Drug-war-based foreign interventions must be fully delegitimized. Just as the UN successfully delegitimized colonialism, so too must it delegitimize drug-war intervention. The two most well-known projects of this type, the US's adventures in Colombia and the ongoing one in Mexico, have proven to be deadly, unmitigated disasters. Well over 200,000 deaths, with no discernable decline in drug activity, have resulted from these efforts.

5. **Death penalty**. A special case of proportionality, the death penalty for purely drug offenses (as against drug-related murders) must end. UN must push harder on ending the death penalty for drug offenses. Far too many instances of drug-based executions are known to be motivated by political considerations, rather than the alleged drug-based wrongdoing. Moreover, the UN high command has long called imposing the death penalty for drug offenses a serious *human rights violation*. Even the US, long the major force behind the international drug war, opposes the death penalty for non-lethal drug crimes.

7

6. **Discrimination**. Discriminatory enforcement of drug laws are shown to exist in many areas. The poor and the marginalized are more often targeted for enforcement than others. Such has clearly been shown to be so in the US, the Philippines, and the UK, while widely suspected of occurring elsewhere. The UN must establish or strengthen prohibitions on discrimination.

7. **Harm reduction.** The UN must push harder to embed the principle of harm reduction into the drug regulatory ideals. For one, encourage moving drug usage reduction efforts from criminal law auspices to health agencies' operations. The latter are better equipped to understand and treat users. Studies have repeatedly shown that treatment works better than incarceration and costs far less. Low-level drug dealers and couriers also merit alternatives to harsh punishment, as many engage in these practices because of poverty or coercion by organized traffickers. Yet, many have been executed for such acts.

8. **Human rights.** The UN should condemn all penalties for mere possession. Millions use many drugs without harming themselves or others. Criminalizing them is a blatant violation of human rights and breeds disrespect for law. Likewise, entering homes against residents' will, conducting random frisks and bodily searches, or displacing village residents while pursuing traffickers, are all violations of human rights standards and merit vociferous condemnation.

9. **Enforcement**. The UN should encourage states wishing to retain the enforcement approach to focus only on organized crime traffickers, not those who merely use. In addition, they should rely on scientifically sound measures to indicate progress and should weigh those gains against the harms the activities may cause with an eye toward considering modifications.

10. **Recognition**. The UN should provide far more recognition, and should more widely promulgate, the successes achieved by the states which have decriminalized or legalized drug-related activities. While many have merited such recognition, the example of Portugal should especially be elevated to prominence with strong UN endorsement as a model for the entire world.

Key Resources

Boullosa, C. and Wallace, M. (2015) *A Narco History: How the United States and Mexico Jointly Created the "Mexican Drug War."* New York: OR Books.

Eastwood, N., Fox, E. and and Rosmarin, A. (2016) *A Quiet Revolution: Drug Decriminalization across the Globe.* London, Release. Retrieved Dec 11, 2017 (https://www.release.org.uk/publications/drug-decriminalisation-2016).

Gallahue, P. (2015) *Drugs and the Death Penalty.* New York: Open Society Foundations. Retrieved Dec. 11, 2017 (https://www.opensocietyfoundations.org/reports/drugs-and-death-penalty).

Global Commission on Drug Policy (2016) *Advancing Drug Policy Reform: A New Approach to Decriminalization.* Retrieved Dec. 11, 2017 (http://www.globalcommissionondrugs.org/reports/advancing-drug-policy-reform/).

Greenwald, G. (ed) (2009) *Drug Decriminalization in Portugal: Lessons for Creating Fair and Successful Drug Policies.* Washington, DC: The Cato Institute.

Kristof, N. (2017) How to Win a War on Drugs. *New York Times.* September 22. Retrieved Dec.22, 2017 (https://www.nytimes.com/2017/09/22/opinion/sunday/portugal-drug-decriminalization.html?_r=0).

Latin American Commission on Drugs and Democracy (2009) *Drugs and Democracy: Toward a Paradigm Shift: Statement by the Latin American Commission on Drugs and Democracy.* Retrieved Dec. 11, 2017 (http://www.globalcommissionondrugs.org/wp-content/uploads/2016/06/drugs-and-democracy_statement_EN.pdf).

McCoy, A.W. (2003) (1972) *The Politics of Heroin: CIA Complicity in the Global Drug Trade: Afghanistan, Southeast Asia, Central America, Colombia.* Revised edition. Chicago: Lawrence Hill Books.

Paley, D. (2014) *Drug War Capitalism.* Chico, CA: AK Press.

Rolles, S. (2009) *After the War on Drugs: Blueprint for Regulation.* UK: Transforming Drug Policy Foundation. Retrieved Dec. 15, 2017 (www.tdpf.org.uk/sites/default/files/Blueprint.pdf).

Sinha, J. (2001) *The History and Development of the Leading International Drug Control Conventions.* February 21. Retrieved Dec.11, 2017 (https://sencanada.ca/content/sen/committee/371/ille/library/history-e.htm#ABSTRACT).

US Department of Justice Drug Enforcement Administration (2017) 2017 National Drug Threat Assessment. DEAIntelPublications@usdoj.gov. Retrieved Dec 21, 2017 (https://www.dea.gov/docs/DIR-040-17_2017-NDTA.pdf).

TWO

Global Police Discrimination

Craig A. Boylstein, Coastal Carolina University

The Problem

Discrimination in policing is an ongoing social problem around the world, affecting the public health and safety of group members (e.g., racial and ethnic marginalized groups, members of the LGBTQ community, drug users, and younger members of specific religious sects) who are disproportionately impacted by police actions. Discrimination in policing is a broad term that may involve the targeting of specific neighborhoods for increased police surveillance. Increased surveillance of specific populations increases arrest rates in those neighborhoods compared to other neighborhoods in the district even though rates of petty theft, drug distribution, and drug use are similar across neighborhoods. For example, discrimination in policing may involve targeting specific groups of people for stop-and-frisk actions without any legally justifiable cause to do so. The stop-and-frisk policy in New York City is one example where officers temporarily detain, question, and at times, search civilians for weapons and other illegal items. Such procedures are not unconstitutional when an officer stops and frisks an individual if the officer has a reasonable suspicion that the person has committed, is committing, or is about to commit a crime. This procedure peaked in 2011 with New Yorkers stopped 685,724 times, with 605,328 (89%) being totally innocent of any wrongdoing. Of those stopped, 55% were black, 32% Latino, and 11% white. Although the practice of stop-and-frisk has decreased in recent years, of the 12,404 New Yorkers stopped in 2016, 9,394 were totally innocent (76%), with 52% of those stopped black, 29% Latino and 10% white.

Another example of discrimination in policing can be seen in disproportionately higher arrest rates for specific racial/ethnic groups for a criminal activity at the local, state, and/or national level, in which all racial/ethnic groups have a generally equal likelihood of engaging in the activity. For example, although black and white Americans use marijuana at approximately the same rate, black Americans are 3.73 times more likely than white Americans to be arrested for marijuana possession. While disproportionate stops, searches, and arrests are examples of over-policing (increased surveillance and control) the same racial minority-dominant neighborhoods that are over-policed often simultaneously experience under-policing. Under-policing is when a specific community receives fewer preventive and support police services compared to overall society. One recent study found majority black resident police precincts in St. Louis, Missouri are more likely to undercount rape compared to local police precincts that serve fewer black residents, largely due to a lack of victim support and slower investigative procedures.

Another form of discrimination in policing involves higher rates of force used against specific groups of civilians, ranging from higher rates of disrespect including being cursed at to higher rates of unarmed deaths caused by police officers' use of force. While there is a robust literature in the U.S. on police discrimination, it is also a worldwide phenomenon. For example, in the Brazilian cities of Rio de Janeiro and Sao Paulo, where the proportion of black and "mulatto" civilians killed by police is higher than their respective population share. The fatal shooting of black and mulatto Brazilians is particularly high in low-income neighborhoods (favelas) that surround Rio de Janeiro and Sao Paulo. In France, urban zones (*banlieues*) that surround cities such as Paris and Marseille that are deemed "high-risk" for crime by the state are areas that receive consistent reports of police harassment and higher rates of use-of-force against minority youth. Most reports of police discrimination in Brazilian favelas and French banlieues continue to be ignored by the state and its police representatives.

Forms of discrimination in policing often result in life-altering consequences not only for the victim, but also the victim's family members, friends, and other members of the victim's community. One example can be seen in the story of the daughter of Eric Garner, Erica Garner, who died on December 30, 2017 because of complications from a massive heart attack. She was an outspoken advocate for police reform since her father's death in 2014. Even after recommendations of "stiff punishment" for the officer who had choked her father, he was put on desk duty from the time of the incident and was no longer issued with a firearm, yet received substantial pay increases, earning $120,000 during the 2016 fiscal year. On December, 30 2017, Erica Garner died at age 27. Reading posts placed on her Twitter page immediately upon the news of her cardiac arrest, coma, and ultimately, her passing, many of Erica's followers (and the person with access to the account throughout this time) noted the stress and complete frustration she felt over her father's death, largely concluding that the continued stress and frustration was a crucial factor in her heart attack. For one example of her pain and frustration, after learning of the pay increase for the officer seen in the publicly available video placing her father in a "chokehold" prior to Mr. Garner's death, Erica Tweeted: "This seems like movies. A bad one. No justice, no records, mayor tells me all lives matter. Pantaleo gets a bonus." To see online footage of your father being choked to death (as Erica noted she had experienced), with the officer never indicted for the killing, and learning that the officer now earns substantially more money from the city than he had earned prior to the fatal incident, only increases the stress that family members of victims of police violence must live with. Victims of police violence who survive the incident, such as Rodney King, often die prematurely, suffering from post-traumatic stress disorder as well as the physical complications that result from the incident. It has been discovered that perceived police discrimination based on one's group identity characteristics increases rates of generalized anxiety disorder for members of specific racial groups.

In the United States, Brazil, and France, the impact of racial and ethnic discrimination in policing and how each country's history of racism influences modern-day policing practices is not only a running theme in the academic literature but has recently gained worldwide attention in various forms of popular media. One example is the #BlackLivesMatter movement. The movement was formed to challenge racially biased, discriminatory policing practices, and to pursue racial justice more largely. #BlackLivesMatter initially arose on social media in 2013 after the acquittal of George Zimmerman in the shooting death of Trayvon Martin but became nationally recognized following street demonstrations of two 2014 police killings of unarmed African-American men, Michael Brown (Ferguson, MO) and Eric Garner (New York City). It was the 2015 killing of Freddie Gray in Baltimore, Maryland that sparked an international movement protesting racial police discrimination around the world, sometimes called the "Black Spring," referencing its relationship with another international protest, the Arab Spring. Over recent years #BlackLivesMatter protests have occurred in Melbourne, Australia to protest the mistreatment of Aboriginal Australians; in Toronto, Ontario to protest the police killings of Andrew Loku and Jermain Carby; and in London, where protestors blocked London's Heathrow Airport on August 4, 2016 in conjunction with protests in the English cities of Birmingham and Nottingham marking the five-year anniversary of the police killing of Mark Duggan. #BlackLivesMatter supporters again protested in London on June 25, 2017 to demand justice for Edson Da Costa, who had died while in police custody, reportedly from a severe reaction to CS spray. The protests in Melbourne, Toronto, and England are only a few examples of the international protests of discrimination in policing. #BlackLivesMatter protests have occurred in Ireland, Netherlands, Germany, South Africa, France, Brazil, and Ghana. The #BlackLivesMatter movement has also served as a spark for other protest movements such as the worldwide #NotInMyName movement that protested the increase in Muslim deaths in India during the first six months of 2017. Those deaths largely resulted from "private militias," members of which referred to themselves as "Gau Rakshaks" (cow protectionists). While these private militias were not sanctioned by the state, Indian prime minister, Narendra Modi, did not publicly speak out against the Gau Rakshaks until after the #NotInMyName protest took place. The protest occurred on June 28th, 2017, with Prime Minister Modi responding the following day on Twitter, stating, "Killing people in the name of Gau Bhakti is not acceptable."

Research Evidence

There are numerous forms of police discrimination that occur throughout the world. One example is rural-to-urban migrants inside of China who report experiencing police discrimination, particularly as part of the household program (*hukou*) that restricts the movements, rights, and social benefits of rural migrants. When rural-to-urban migrants are victims of crime, they report being ignored by police officers, with cases never being investigated. HIV/AIDS advocates and other members of the LGBT community have also reported being discriminated against by Chinese police. For example, a "raid" on March 30, 2009 by Guangzhou police at Renmin Gongyuan People's Park reported that 60 gay men were arrested, allegedly for prostitution, although many of those arrested were part of an HIV/AIDs outreach program. Approximately 20% of transgender people living in Beijing report having been arrested with approximately 50% reporting being threatened by police. Another group that is marginalized in China is intravenous drug users, who disproportionately report being questioned and interrogated by police even when they have broken no laws. Russian, Ukrainian, Chilean, and Canadian police have also been reported of harassing and disproportionately detaining ethnic minorities, intravenous drug users, and members of the LGBT community.

Additionally, the discrimination found in policing outcomes among certain racial, ethnic, sexual identity, and drug user groups, often extends to religious minority groups around the world, with members reporting being victims of police surveillance, harassment, and brutality. For example, policing discrimination within Tibet ranges from constant video surveillance not seen in other Chinese provinces, police checkpoints within and around the city of Lhasa, to the arrests and at times, brutalization, of peaceful religious protestors (e.g., the repeated use of a conducted energy device, or CED, on a Buddhist monk, with the CED ultimately placed inside of his mouth and then discharged). In Xinjiang, China, the Uyghur Muslim separatists often receive harsh, violent treatment by Chinese policing authorities sent by the government. Muslims in Berlin, London, and Madrid report being disproportionately stopped and treated disrespectfully by police, particularly those under the age of 35, with younger Muslims being twice as likely to report police discrimination compared to older Muslims. Conflicts between Buddhists and Muslims in countries such as Thailand, Myanmar (Burma), and Sri Lanka, have resulted in mob violence against Muslims that goes unpunished by police and declarations of martial law by state authorities in areas in which Muslims are protesting unfair treatment (e.g., the burning of mosques that go uninvestigated by local police authorities).

Young Latinos living in New York City report being victims of aggressive police tactics (e.g., stop-and-frisk) that restrict and criminalize Latino youths' use of public urban space. Like young Muslims reporting higher rates of police harassment compared to older Muslims living in European cities, younger Aboriginal people in Australia report much higher rates of police discrimination than do older Aboriginal people. Ultimately, black civilians, members of ethnic minorities, LGBT members, rural-to-urban migrants, religious minorities, intravenous drug users, and Aboriginals all report forms of police discrimination that can be linked to over-policing around the world.

One outcome of over-policing is disproportionate arrest rates for targeted groups. For example, the likelihood of arrest is approximately 20 times higher for indigenous Australians compared to non-indigenous Australians. This difference in arrest rates across ethnic groups in Australia has been linked to over-policing practices such as higher numbers of police being stationed in indigenous predominant neighborhoods and much less discretion used in arresting indigenous citizens for public order offending (e.g., drinking in public). It has been found that young black (in U.S. and Canada) and Latino (U.S.) men are vastly over-represented in terms of who gets stopped and frisked by police. Data indicate that members of these groups are no more likely to possess illegal firearms or illicit drugs than other citizens. When members of targeted groups are stopped at rates as high as 10:1; however, the arrests also become disproportionate compared to the level of offenses across race/ethnic groups. That is, white Canadians, Americans, Australians, French people, Brazilians, and English people are stopped less frequently, resulting in a lower arrest rate compared to members of racial/ethnic minority groups. Thus, over-policing certain groups of people results in extended negative outcomes such as higher rates of arrest and imprisonment, which can impact employment and educational opportunities.

While over-policing young minority group members is a fundamental problem around the world, the concept of under-policing is also important. Under-policing can be referred to as police neglect. One example involves Arab women in Israel who report being victims of domestic violence that goes uninvestigated by local police. Another is the lack of investigations into sexual assaults that occur in rural parts of India. The killings of Muslims by the Gau Rakshaks in India was at least partially perpetuated by under-policing since the killers went unpunished, were not investigated, nor arrested for their crimes. Like Aboriginal Australians, Native Americans are victims of over-policing when it comes to public order offending such as public drunkenness, but victims of under-policing when it comes to being subjects of physical assault, sexual assault, and homicide.

A study of five Belgian cities found that police over-police "regular customers", people who tend to have weak social networks, lack the ability to care for themselves, and live in marginalized housing conditions. Police develop nicknames for these "regular customers," such as "drunks", "petty crooks", "jerks", "tramps", and "amoebas," which are used to quickly communicate complex social phenomena, helping officers to predict the behavior of the individuals they encounter, adjusting intervention strategies according to which group an individual is identified with. Groups found to be under-policed included transients (travelers, students, gypsies), who find police will not help when they are victimized (e.g., have a bike stolen; are a victim of sexual assault). A second group of under-policed Belgian residents were long-term residents who preferred to manage their problems without police assistance. The two social groups best fitting that description were Turkish and Pakistani residents. A third group under-policed were recent immigrants from Eastern Europe, whom the police did not feel comfortable dealing with, feeling a social "distance" from them.

Research on discrimination in policing around the world indicates a complex web of over-policing and under-policing strategies sometimes with distinct groups within the same community (the example discussed from Belgium) and other times within the same social group. This worldwide system of over-policing and under-policing is the basis for discrimination found within criminal justice systems stretching from the Americas through Europe, Africa, Asia, and the South Pacific. The issue becomes how these practices and outcomes can be reduced, and hopefully, eliminated.

Recommendations and Solutions

Commonalities exist in what kinds of discriminatory practices are found in policing across the world (over-policing/under-policing certain groups), which leads to straightforward recommendations and solutions. These universal recommendations include the following.

- End stop-and-frisk practices, as they disproportionately impact young minority males and result in no reduction in crime. New York City reported its lowest crime rate in recorded history in 2017, despite phasing out its stop-and-frisk policy.
- Eliminate arrests for petty crimes. Some examples include Mexico's 2009 decriminalization of personal amounts of drugs (*narcomenudeo*); the New Zealand Prostitute's Collective (NZPC); there are a few U.S. cities and at least eight countries that do not arrest or charge for drinking in public; likewise, there are many countries where loitering is not a crime. Strict petty-crime laws lead to over-policing specific groups (i.e., ethnic/racial minorities and homeless citizens), generating high arrest records for these social groups.
- Implement community policing techniques including "checking-in" on residents to ensure there have been no un-reported criminal incidents. Adopted from the Japanese Koban system, such a system was implemented in Singapore and is a tremendous success. They set up neighborhood police posts with part of officer responsibilities involving making house visits to develop rapport and trust among officers and residents.
- Increase accountability for officers with multiple use-of-force complaints and/or those involved in a fatal encounter of an unarmed

civilian. The countries of England, Belgium, New Zealand, and Wales all have an independent police conduct authority that handles misconduct complaints. The European Union (EU) has established national police monitoring and inspection bodies and Anti-corruption agencies for each full EU member country. Canada has an extensive list of complaint commissions, review boards, response teams, and investigative offices.

- A better balance in training hours for lower forms of force and higher levels of force (CEDs, firearms) result in lower civilian fatalities. Many countries around the world implement such training procedures, including Great Britain and many in the EU (Germany, Spain, Norway, Sweden). One example is Iceland, where there is a high proportion of gun ownership and a strong citizen gun culture but very little gun violence. Icelandic police training emphasizes peaceful de-escalation and limited reliance on firearms in training officers. Only one person has been killed by police in all of Iceland's history.

In terms of social movements such as #BlackLivesMatter, the group drew up a list of 40 policy recommendations, including demilitarization of the police, an end to money bail, ending deportations, passing state and federal legislation that requires the U.S. to acknowledge the lasting impacts of slavery and to execute a plan to address those impacts. Global issues involve economic justice including affordable housing, demanding the right to restored land, clean air, and clean water. As global economic leaders prepare to meet in 2018 for the G20 summit, the group's agenda priorities for the meeting of increasing access to quality job training, generating sustainable infrastructure projects, and improving the quality of global food management touch on at least some aspects of the #BlackLivesMatter larger agenda. As the President of Argentina stated "this is the moment when we must renew our commitments with the broader goal of leaving no one behind. This is the moment to build new bridges across the globe." There certainly is a need for global economic and social reform on multiple fronts as the March 14, 2018 assassination of Rio de Janeiro city council member, sociologist, and human rights activist Marielle Franco illustrates. Franco was a noted outspoken critic of police corruption and advocate for favela residents. She was known for her popular phrase "We are together," and just days before her murder called for "no more killing of young men," criticizing Brazilian police for their corruption and overt brutality. Now is the time for each of us to continue Marielle

Franco's struggle. Now is the time for each of us who believe in the importance of justice to demand it for all global citizens.

Key Resources

Adelman, M., Erez, E. and Shalhoub-Kevorkian, N. (2003) Policing violence against minority women in multicultural societies: "Community" and the politics of exclusion, *Police & Society*, 7.

Body-Gendrot, S. (2010) Police marginality, racial logics and discrimination in the banlieues of France, *Ethnic and Racial Studies*, 33(4), 656-674.

Brownlow, A. (2018) The Uneven Geographies of America's Hidden Rape Crisis: A District-Level Analysis of Underpolicing in St. Louis. *Annals of the American Association of Geographers*, 108(2), 411-423.

Brüß, J. (2008) Experiences of discrimination reported by Turkish, Moroccan and Bangladeshi Muslims in three European cities, *Journal of Ethnic and Migration Studies*, 34(6), 875-894.

Cano, I. (2010) Racial bias in police use of lethal force in Brazil, *Police Practice and Research: An International Journal*, 11(1), 31-43.

Cunneen, C. (2001) *Conflict, Politics and Crime: Aboriginal Communities and the Police*, Sydney: Allen and Unwin. Available at SSRN: https://ssrn.com/abstract=2196235

Easton, M. (2014) 'Blind spot' policing in Belgian multicultural neighbourhoods and the implications for human rights, *Australian Journal of Human Rights*, 20(2), 19-39.

Huguet, C. and Szabó de Carvalho, I. (2008). Violence in the Brazilian Favelas and the Role of the Police, *New Directions for Student Leadership*, 2008 (119), 93-109.

Mimiaga, M.J., Safren, S.A., Dvoryak, S., Reisner, S.L., Needle, R. and Woody, G. (2010). "We fear the police, and the police fear us": Structural and individual barriers and facilitators to HIV medication adherence among injection drug users in Kiev, Ukraine, *AIDS care*, 22(11), 1305-1313.

Perry, B. (2009) *Policing race and place in Indian Country: Over-and underenforcement*, Lexington Books.

Solis, C., Portillos, E.L. and Brunson, R.K. (2009) Latino youths' experiences with and perceptions of involuntary police encounters. *The Annals of the American Academy of Political and Social Science*, 623(1), 39-51.

Soto, J.A., Dawson-Andoh, N.A. and BeLue, R. (2011) The relationship between perceived discrimination and generalized anxiety disorder among African Americans, Afro Caribbeans, and non-Hispanic Whites, *Journal of anxiety disorders*, 25(2), 258-265.

Taylor, K.Y. (2016) *From# BlackLivesMatter to black liberation*, Haymarket Books.

THREE

Wrongful Convictions and Exonerations: Global Data Sources and Other Initiatives

Tereza Trejbalová and Terance D. Miethe,
University of Nevada, Las Vegas

The Problem

Criminal justice systems across the world provide various safeguards to reduce the risk of wrongful convictions of the innocent. These safeguards involve basic legal principles (e.g., presumption of innocence, "beyond a reasonable doubt" standards of guilt), constitutional rights of the accused (e.g., the right to legal counsel, cross-examination of witnesses), and professional standards (e.g., guidelines for prosecutorial and judicial conduct). Nevertheless, these safeguards sometimes fail to protect the innocent from human errors of omission and commission. Despite major growth in these legal protections over the last half-century, wrongful convictions remain a serious threat to our basic views about justice. These errors are especially tragic when they are recognized only after long prison commitment or death of the falsely accused. Even when exonerations occur over a shorter time period and have less than lethal consequences, there is often irrevocable harm to the persons involved and their families.

Many countries and organizations dedicate their time and resources to identify and rectify wrongful convictions. These entities also provide some indication of the nature, causes, and socio-geographical distribution of wrongful convictions. Unfortunately, comparisons of these patterns and trends across data sources and nations are often difficult because of: (1) the use of different legal criteria for defining exonerations and wrongful convictions across data sources; (2) differences in the comprehensiveness of the data collection; and (3) the lack of available data on these cases across many world regions.

The current paper is designed to summarize what we know about the nature and distribution of the primary causal factors associated with wrongful convictions (e.g. the fallibility of eyewitness testimony or third-party testimonies). It briefly describes the most comprehensive data sources currently available on this topic within and across world regions, and concludes with a discussion on the growth of international initiatives and standards to help minimize the prevalence of wrongful convictions.

Research Evidence

Definitional Issues

Exonerations are defined as occurrences "when a person who has been convicted of a crime is officially cleared based on new evidence of innocence" (National Registry Exonerations n.d.). Wrongful conviction is what precedes an exoneration—it is a conviction that is based on flawed proceedings that have omitted indications of legal, actual/factual innocence, or both types of innocence. Before proceeding with a discussion on different data sources for exonerations, the distinction between actual/factual legal and innocence must be highlighted.

Actual or factual innocence refers to cases in which individuals did not commit the crime they were arrested for and convicted of (Hoffman 2007). These individuals are the "super category of innocence" (Raymond 2001: 457) because they are actually innocent of the crime but were wrongfully convicted of it. In contrast, reversible errors during trial can lead to a release of an individual due to procedural errors. These events are termed legal innocence, and they suggest that an individual may have committed a crime; however, the trial was conducted in an inadequate way and hence the sentence was overturned (Strutin 2011).

Primary Causes of Wrongful Convictions

Research on exonerations and wrongful convictions suggests that there are several factors that contribute to their occurrence. The following is a summary of the most commonly discussed reasons.

Forensic evidence

The link between flawed forensic evidence and wrongful conviction is widely recognized in previous research (e.g., Gould et al. 2014; Huff 2004). Wrongful convictions from dubious forensics may be a result of unintentional human error that occurred during the proceedings or intentional misconduct committed by prosecutors and experts (e.g., Gould et al. 2014). Intentional misconduct is the most commonly investigated category, because implication of certain individuals may be deliberately committed by the officials that are meant to pursue justice (Huff 2004).

Third-party testimonies

Several parties can provide a third-party testimony, such as jailhouse informants, accomplices and other witnesses (Roth 2016). Jailhouse informants, for example, are defined as informants in custody that provide information on another defendant's crime in hopes of receiving advantages for this secondary information (Winograde 1990). These testimonies have been found in some studies to be more influential in case outcome than direct eyewitness and other types of testimonies (Wetmore, Neuschatz and Gronlund 2014). Their influence has also been shown to be unaffected by the disclosure of the informant's testimony history (Neuschatz et al. 2012).

Eyewitness testimony issues

The source of eyewitness testimony can be divided into several categories. These include photo lineups, live lineups, mug shot search, and spontaneous identifications and naming (Levi and Levi 2013). Wells and Olson (2003) note that an eyewitness testimony is often "the only evidence available for determining the identity of the culprit" (p. 277). While such statement suggests that faulty eyewitness testimony is one of the most common factors underlying exonerations and acquittals, Levi and Levi (2013) find that eyewitness testimonies were relatively sparse within the Innocence Project cases.

Official misconduct

Misconduct by officials is a special category because it inherently contains a discussion on the ethics of criminal justice decision makers (Joy 2006). The most frequently discussed type of official misconduct is prosecutorial misconduct (e.g., Krieger 2011; Perlin 2016). Prosecutors have to work and function in a stressful environment that may contribute to them pursuing high conviction rates, regardless of their ethical reasoning (Krieger 2011). Consequently, serious prosecutorial misconduct, such as Brady violations when the state withholds evidence from the defense, is among the primary reasons for a sentence reversal or vacation (Perlin 2016).

Recommendations and Solutions

Previous studies have suggested several recommendations and solutions to the worldwide problem of wrongful convictions in the criminal justice systems. As described below, there are two ways this problem is being addressed: (1) providing systematic data on wrongful convictions and exonerations exemplifying the magnitude of the problem for policy planning; and (2) practical implementation of these data by governmental and non-governmental organizations.

Comprehensive Data Collection

Various organizations across the world have recognized cases of wrongful convictions. However, systematic data that consistently report and record the nature and prevalence of these practices are generally lacking. Such data are necessary to address this basic problem in criminal justice systems across the world. The best available data sources on cases of innocence and wrongful convictions are summarized below.

Global sources

The *Innocence Network* involves 69 organizations over the world dedicated to "providing pro bono legal and investigative services to individuals seeking to prove innocence of crimes for which they have been convicted, and working to redress the causes of wrongful convictions" (Innocence Network n.d.). Although not all these member organizations provide information on exonerees, they all share the goal of the dissemination of resources and information.

Several of these organizations provide specific information on individual cases. For example, the *Irish Innocence Project at Griffith College* provides information on two exonerees in Ireland. The *Knoops' Innocence Project* in the Netherlands reports currently working on 25 cases, and identifies seven individuals whose exonerations were tied directly to the organization's work. In Asia, the *Taiwan Innocence Project* includes eight cases of actual innocence exonerated in the country. *Innocence Canada* reports that 21 cases of exonerations are directly connected to this organization and is currently working on 86 additional cases.

Wrongful Convictions Blog is a media outlet that provides updates on wrongful convictions and exonerations across the world. It includes a large database containing articles, resources and news from international websites that address wrongful convictions. This global source serves as a crucial addition to the discourse on exonerations as it provides an international scope that is unprecedented by regional organizations.

Amnesty International (AI) focuses specifically on death penalty exonerations. This organization reported 71 exonerations in six countries in 2015 and 60 exonerations in nine countries in 2016. However, AI data lacks specific details about the exonerated individuals. The organization focus on situations of legal innocence as they claim "exoneration is the process whereby, after sentencing and the conclusion of the appeals process, the convicted person is later cleared from blame or acquitted of the criminal charge, and therefore is regarded as innocent in the eyes of the law" (Amnesty International 2017: 6).

Finally, *International Network for Innocent Arson Defendants* specializes and provides support to defendants in arson cases. It focuses on two general types of cases: "(1) Arson Denied (i.e., fires which were accidental, and the conviction was based on junk science and/or investigative malfeasance) and (2) Wrongfully Convicted (i.e., fires were set but the police charged the wrong party to clear the case quickly, to protect the real perpetrator, or to convict someone they do not like)" (NIAD n.d.). The organization focuses on cases of actual innocence and its database contains 22 individuals from three countries (USA, Germany, and Japan) who were either exonerated, released through a plea bargain, parole, or are waiting for a retrial.

Regional sources

It is apparent that international databases providing information on wrongful convictions and exonerations are extremely scarce. Some of the international member organizations of the Innocence Network provide data on individuals who were directly helped by their projects. However, based on this research, comprehensive databases are lacking across most world regions.

In Latin America, *Red Inocente* was founded in 2014 to provide support for innocence projects and organizations in this region. The organization is based at California Western School of Law in San Diego and operates under the auspices of the California Innocent Project. As of December 2017, the organization reports 17 exonerees in Mexico, four exonerees in Puerto Rico, two in Colombia, three in Chile, four in Argentina, two in Peru, two in Bolivia, one in Ecuador, and two in Nicaragua. The organization provides detailed information on the exonerees (e.g., offender/offense attributes).

One of the most exhaustive regional sources is *INNOCENT* in the UK. As of December 2017, this database contains information on 135 actually innocent exonerees. In contrast, The U.S.–Asia Law Institute's *Wrongful Convictions Database* was established to examine Chinese wrongful convictions, but only one case is contained in this database as of December 2017.

National sources

Different organizations in the US have slightly different lists of exonerated individuals depending on the organization's specialization. The *National Registry of Exonerations* (NRE) provides the largest database of exonerees to date (2107) because it includes all types of crimes. Based on the organization's definition, the database focuses on cases of actual innocence. NRE's database is not an exhaustive source due to time and personnel restrictions, as well as the possibility of undiscovered cases.

The work of the *Innocence Project* (IP) goes beyond the identification and reporting of particular cases. Since 1992, the IP actively works on the reform of the criminal justice system through DNA testing and offering litigation services. As of October 2017, the Innocence Project reports 351 DNA exonerations and subsequent identification of 150 real perpetrators. This database is not limited to death row inmates or even defendants convicted of murder. However, due to their focus on DNA testing many of the cases include other violent crimes (e.g., rape, robbery).

The *Death Penalty Information Center* (DPIC) only includes individuals exonerated from the death row in the US since 1973. To be included in the DPIC database, the following characteristics must be present:

> Defendants must have been convicted, sentenced to death and subsequently either – a. Been acquitted of all charges related to the crime that placed them on death row, or b. Had all charges related to the crime that placed them on death row dismissed by the prosecution or the courts, or c. Been granted a complete pardon based on evidence of innocence. (DPIC n.d.)

The DPIC's explanation of the necessity to include only individuals legally exempt from guilt suggests that it focuses solely on legal innocence. In practice, this means that some cases that are included in the Death Penalty Information Center are not included in the NRE database due to differing definitions of innocence.

Global Initiatives and Standards

Aside from providing relevant and transparent data to extend public awareness about wrongful convictions, governmental and non-governmental entities are fundamental in developing and implementing several practices to help resolve this problem.

Governmental agencies

There are several countries where wrongful convictions are being addressed by enhancing their system of checks and balances. In particular, Bangladesh, China, Ghana, Kuwait, Mauritania, Nigeria, Sudan, Taiwan, and Vietnam reported exonerated death row inmates in 2016 (Amnesty International 2017). While most of the specific member organizations of the Innocence Network are located within the United States, there are also member organizations in Argentina, Australia, Canada, Ireland, Israel, Italy, the Netherlands, New Zealand, Taiwan, and the UK. The geographical location of the majority of these countries suggests that First-World/Westernized countries implement mechanisms to protect innocent individuals more frequently. Other entities (e.g., the International Network for Innocent Arson Defendants) have a far more limited scope of international coverage. As a legal means of financial redress for the wrongfully convicted, The *United Nations* (UN) specifically proposes compensation for these victims through Article 14 (6)[1] in the *International Covenant on Civil and Political Rights*. Similarly, the EU attempts to compensate these victims through *Protocol No. 7* to the *European Convention for the Protection of Human Rights and Fundamental Freedoms* Article 3[2]. Given that these documents are not legally binding, the membership states themselves are the sole decision makers on the matter, unless the case reaches the European Court of Human Rights in the case of the European Union.

Non-governmental agencies

Aside from providing legal and investigative services to the wrongfully convicted, the Innocence Network also organizes annual *International Wrongful Conviction Day* (October 2, 2017). This day is designed to raise awareness through the organization of different events. In 2017, the Innocence Network held a virtual event on Facebook, and several NBA players commented on the issue. Since it is recognized that even innocent individuals are stigmatized once they return to the mainstream society, the Innocence Network also includes organizations such as *After Innocence* located in California. After Innocence provides the wrongfully convicted with assistance after their exoneration. International re-entry

---

[1] "When a person has by a final decision been convicted of a criminal offence and when subsequently his conviction has been reversed or he has been pardoned on the ground that a new or newly discovered fact shows conclusively that there has been a miscarriage of justice, the person who has suffered punishment as a result of such conviction shall be compensated according to law, unless it is proved that the non-disclosure of the unknown fact in time is wholly or partly attributable to him" (United Nations 1966: 177).

[2] The wording of Article 14(6) in the International Covenant on Civil and Political Rights and Article 3 of Protocol No. 7 to the European Convention for the Protection of Human Rights and Fundamental Freedoms are nearly identical.

organizations for wrongfully convicted individuals are not present in the Innocence Network.

References

Amnesty International (2017) *Death Sentences and Executions 2016.* Retrieved Nov. 23, 2017 (https://www.amnesty.org/en/documents/act50/5740/2017/en/).

Council of Europe (1950) *Convention for the Protection of Human Rights and Fundamental Freedoms.* Retrieved Dec. 1, 2017 (http://www.echr.coe.int/Documents/Convention_ENG.pdf).

Death Penalty Information Center (n.d.) The Innocence List, Retrieved Nov. 15, 2017 (https://deathpenaltyinfo.org/innocence-list-those-freed-death-row).

Gould, J.B., Carrano, J., Leo, R.A. and Hail-Jares, K. (2014) Predicting Erroneous Convictions, *Iowa Law Review*, 99: 471-522.

Hoffman, M.B. (2007) The Myth of Factual Innocence, *Chicago-Kent Law Review*, 82: 663-690.

Huff, R.C. (2004) Wrongful Convictions: The American Experience, *Canadian Journal of Criminology and Criminal Justice*, 46: 107-120.

The Innocence Network (n.d.) Retrieved Dec. 23, 2017 (http://innocencenetwork.org).

International Network for Innocent Arson Defendants (n.d.) Retrieved Dec. 22, 2017 (http://www.niad.info/About.html).

Joy, P.A (2006) The Relationship between Prosecutorial Misconduct and Wrongful convictions: Shaping Remedies for a Broken System., *Wisconsin Law Review*, 2006: 399-429.

Krieger, S.A. (2011) Why Our Justice System Convicts Innocent People, and the Challenges Faced by Innocence Projects Trying to Exonerate Them, *New Criminal Law Review: An International and Interdisciplinary Journal*, 14: 333-402.

Levi, A. and Levi, J. (2013) The Role of Eyewitness Testimony in Exonerations: An Archival Study, *The Open Law Journal*, 5(1): 1-9.

Neuschatz, J.S., Wilkinson, M.L., Goodsell, C.A., Wetmore, S.A., Quinlivan, D.S. and Jones, N.J. (2012) Secondary Confessions, Expert Testimony, and Unreliable Testimony, *Journal of Police and Criminal Psychology*, 27(2): 179-192.

Perlin, M.L. (2016) 'Merchants and Thieves, Hungry for Power':

Prosecutorial Misconduct and Passive Judicial Complicity in Death Penalty Trials of Defendants with Mental Disabilities, *Washington and Lee Law Review*, 73: 1501-1545.

Raymond, M. (2001) The Problem with Innocence, *Cleveland State Law Review*, 49: 449-463.

Roth, J.A. (2016) Informant Witnesses and the Risk of Wrongful Convictions, *American Criminal Law Review* 53(3): 737-798.

Strutin, K. (2011) The Age of Innocence: Actual, Legal and Presumed, *Law and Technology Resources for Legal Professionals*, Retrieved Dec. 15, 2017 (https://www.llrx.com/2011/05/the-age-of-innocence-actual-legal-and-presumed/).

United Nations (1966) *International Covenant on Civil and Political Rights.* Retrieved Nov. 12, 2017(https://treaties.un.org/doc/publication/unts/volume%20999/volume-999-i-14668-english.pdf).

Wells, G.L. and Olson. E.A. (2003) Eyewitness Testimony, *Annual Review of Psychology*, 54(1): 277–295.

Wetmore, S.A., Neuschatz, J.S. and Gronlund, S.D. (2014) On the Power of Secondary Confession Evidence, *Psychology, Crime & Law*, 20(4): 339-357.

Winograde, J. (1990) Jailhouse Informants and the Need for Judicial Use Immunity in Habeas Corpus Proceedings, *California Law Review*, 78(3): 755-785.

Data Sources

After Innocence (http://www.after-innocence.org)

Death Penalty Information Center (https://deathpenaltyinfo.org)

Innocence Canada (https://www.aidwyc.org)

The Innocence Network (http://innocencenetwork.org)

Innocence Network UK (http://www.innocencenetwork.org.uk)

Innocence Project (https://www.innocenceproject.org)

International Network for Innocent Arson Defendants (http://www.niad.info)

Irish Innocence Project at Griffith College (http://www.innocenceproject.ie)

Knoops' Innocence Project (https://knoopsadvocaten.nl/innocence-project/)

The National Registry of Exonerations (https://www.law.umich.edu/special/exoneration/Pages/about.aspx)

RED Inocente (http://redinocente.org)

Taiwan Innocence Project (http://twinnocenceproject.org/news.php?lang=en)

U.S.–Asia Law Institute's Wrongful Convictions Database (https://usali.org/wrongful-convictions-database/)

The Wrongful Convictions Blog (https://wrongfulconvictionsblog.org)

FOUR

Solutions to Ending the Global Social Problem of HIV Criminalization

Carrie Foote, Indiana University Purdue University-Indianapolis[1]
Edwin Bernard, HIV Justice Network
Eric Mykhalovskiy, York University

The Problem

HIV criminalization involves using the criminal law to punish people living with HIV (PLHIV) for engaging in certain activities, most commonly not disclosing one's HIV-positive status to a sex partner, potentially exposing another person to HIV, or allegedly transmitting the virus. It can also involve sentence enhancements for PLHIV who are found guilty of other "crimes," notably sex work or simple assaults such as spitting at, or biting, another person. HIV criminalization is a complex issue that encompasses the process of defining activities as crimes, enforcing laws, and prosecuting particular cases. It raises important concerns about how societies respond to HIV prevention and about the harmful consequences of using the criminal justice system to address public health problems. Examples of HIV criminalization as a global phenomenon include:

- Zimbabwe: A young woman on HIV medications was convicted under an overly broad, vague HIV-specific law that criminalizes "deliberately infecting another person" and received a suspended sentence of five years in prison. Her partner tested HIV-negative.

[1] Corresponding Author: IUPUI 425 University Blvd, CA 303. Indianapolis, IN. 46228. 317.278.8454 foote@iupui.edu

- Singapore: A young man received a year in prison for allegedly exposing another man to HIV while performing oral sex, an act that posed no HIV transmission risk.
- U.S.: A young man on HIV medications, virally suppressed, and therefore unable to transmit HIV sexually, was sentenced to 25 years in prison for a one-time sexual encounter that involved performing oral sex (without a condom) and anal sex with a condom. He was also required to register as a lifetime sex offender.

HIV criminalization dates back to the early years of the pandemic (late 1980s/early 1990s). Laws that specifically criminalize HIV were first enacted at this time and criminal cases related to HIV non-disclosure, exposure and transmission began to be prosecuted first in the U.S. and then Canada. HIV criminalization was partly justified by some policy makers, media, and legal scholars, claiming that it would help reduce HIV transmission. That claim has never been supported by research evidence.

Despite huge advances in the science of HIV transmission risks and harms and in research showing that HIV criminalization has many unintended negative impacts on public health, HIV criminalization continues unabated in many places in the world, leading to human rights violations. In 2008, UNAIDS/UNDP issued a policy brief that called upon governments to strictly limit the criminalization of HIV. Since that time there has been a growing global movement to end HIV criminalization. Local, national, and global organizations, researchers, human rights activists, healthcare providers, public health and legal experts, and PLHIV have reached a broad consensus that HIV criminalization is deeply flawed and does more harm than good. They have raised the following concerns: HIV criminalization is out of step with current scientific research, results in unjust prosecutions of PLHIV, is deeply stigmatizing, has focused primarily on the most marginalized PLHIV, is contrary to public health goals, and causes tremendous individual harms to those charged and/or convicted within the criminal justice system.

Research Evidence

The HIV Justice Network estimates that 68 countries (98 jurisdictions including 29 applicable U.S. states and territories), have adopted laws that specifically allow for HIV criminalization, while prosecutions for HIV non-disclosure, exposure and transmission have been reported in at least 69 countries (117 jurisdictions). Between October 2015 and October 2017, the Network identified at least 228 arrests, prosecutions and/or convictions in 39 countries. The most prosecutions (in descending order) occurred in the U.S., Belarus, Russia, Canada, Zimbabwe, UK, and the Czech Republic.

There have been some successes in repealing or preventing the passage of HIV criminalization laws in Mauritius, Comoros, Brazil and Malawi. Other jurisdictions such as the Netherlands, Denmark, Switzerland, Norway, Colorado and California in the U.S., and Victoria in Australia have achieved near or total HIV decriminalization. Still, HIV-related prosecutions continue to occur and HIV-specific criminal laws continue to be enacted around the world. For example, since 2000, almost 30 sub-Saharan African countries have enacted overly broad HIV criminalization statutes.

Numerous analyses have found that most HIV criminalization laws do not align with current advances in HIV prevention and treatment science. From the late 2000s onward, scientific research began to show the dramatic impact of effective antiretroviral therapy on HIV transmission risks. Recent studies have demonstrated that treatments reduce viral load—the amount of HIV as measured in the blood—to such low levels that PLHIV who are virally suppressed cannot transmit the virus. Laws that criminalize HIV non-disclosure, exposure and transmission have not kept pace with these important scientific advances. They contribute to HIV stigma by exaggerating the risks of HIV transmission, reinforcing inaccurate information about HIV and counteracting public health efforts to stem the epidemic. They also subject PLHIV who have posed no risk of transmission to criminal punishment and deny protective HIV transmission behavior, such as using a condom or having a low or undetectable viral load, as a legal defense.

Additional studies show evidence of the harmful, if unintended, consequences of HIV criminalization. Studies from the U.S. and Canada have found a "chilling effect" on healthcare provider trust and, in some cases, a reluctance to seek HIV testing. Other analyses from Canada show that sensationalized media accounts of HIV-related criminal cases reinforce HIV stigma and promote fear of PLHIV, particularly of those who are racial minorities. The experience and consequences of HIV criminalization, including harsh sentences and imprisonment, pose enormous challenges for PLHIV. HIV criminalization can lead to instability in housing and employment, disclosure of private medical information, risk of partner and/or incarceration violence, loss of friends, family and children, and disruption of care for HIV.

Further, HIV criminalization often focuses on the most marginalized PLHIV, including gay men, people who use drugs, sex workers, racial minorities, migrants and indigenous peoples. Ultimately it exacerbates HIV stigma and discrimination.

HIV criminalization laws may also violate human rights by ignoring key criminal justice principles by, for example, failing to take into account criminal intent or a person's state of mind, the nature of, and actual, harm posed, and proportionate punishment. Knowledge that one is HIV-positive, understands how HIV is transmitted and did not disclose prior to sex is often used as the primary evidence that an HIV-related crime occurred, rather than evidence of criminal intent and/or actual harm. Consequently, HIV criminalization leads to unjust prosecutions by human rights standards as it punishes behavior that neither caused, nor intended to cause, any harm.

As a result, PLHIV risk being overly criminalized in much of the world. Further, the punishments imposed are often grossly disproportionate to any potential or actual harm, with some PLHIV receiving prison sentences for alleged non-disclosure or potential or perceived exposure that are far longer than the equivalent in that jurisdiction for vehicular homicide. In Canada and some U.S. states, convicted PLHIV are placed on sex offender lists, often for life.

Recommendations and Solutions

We have the prevention and treatment interventions to end the HIV pandemic, but we cannot do that if we continue to unjustly criminalize PLHIV. Although there is no single solution to ending HIV criminalization, there is consensus that efforts will be more successful if they meaningfully involve PLHIV, ideally in leadership roles. It is also critical to understand the particular social, cultural and epidemiological contexts in which HIV is criminalized. What works in one jurisdiction may not work in others. Therefore, it is important to have a wide array of strategies, and combine them, when working to end HIV criminalization.

The following solutions to ending the overly broad criminalization of PLHIV have been articulated by numerous local, national and global organizations, researchers, human rights activists, healthcare providers, public health and legal experts, and PLHIV, including such global bodies as UNAIDS, UNDP, the Open Society Institute, the International Planned Parenthood Federation, The Athena Network, and the HIV JUSTICE WORLDWIDE coalition which includes the

Global Network of People Living with HIV, the HIV Justice Network, and the International Community of Women Living with HIV.

1. *Support HIV Criminalization Reform and Repeal Efforts*

- Jurisdictions must not enact new HIV criminal laws and should carefully monitor new legislative efforts and mobilize to reject any efforts to develop such laws.
- Repeal HIV specific criminal laws that criminalize HIV non-disclosure, exposure and transmission, and remove sentence enhancement based on HIV status.
- Severely limit any HIV-related prosecutions under general criminal statutes to those rare cases where intent to transmit, foreseeability of harm, lack of consent and actual transmission can be proven. Such prosecutions should be informed by the latest HIV science and should be harm-based, not risk-of-harm-based.
- Where repeal is not an option, modernize laws by ensuring they are: (1) based on best criminal justice practices of intent and proportionality of harm; (2) reflect advances in HIV science such as low or undetectable viral loads and the nature of HIV as a chronic manageable condition; (3) recognize measures taken to prevent HIV; and (4) apply proportional punishments (e.g., remove punishments that include sex offender lists and consider alternatives to jail time).
- Uphold and enact laws that protect the human rights of PLHIV (e.g., that prohibit employment and housing discrimination and that ensure equal access to prevention and care services).
- Enact less harmful alternatives to criminalization such as a restorative justice model (which focuses on repairing any alleged harm by creating supervised dialogue between the parties involved and resolving differences); diversion programs (which is a type of sentencing allowing the accused to avoid some charges and engage in counseling rather than incarceration); and/or pursue civil lawsuits as opposed to criminal prosecution.
- Recognize that HIV criminalization is often an extension of already existing criminalization (e.g., of sexual minorities, racial/ethnic minority groups, sex workers and people who use drugs) and that combining efforts to end criminalization across groups will lead to improved advocacy. Advocates can, for example, network with other social justice movements such as those addressing racialized mass incarceration, and emphasize the intersecting nature of different forms of criminalization. Ending HIV criminalization will be more successful if advocacy occurs in conjunction with efforts to end the

criminalization of sex workers, sexual minorities, sex outside of marriage, and people who use drugs as they are intersecting forms of stigma and discrimination.

2. *Educate and Provide Guidance for Law Enforcement and Legal Actors*

- Develop accessible materials to assist legal actors (e.g., prosecutors, judges, lawyers) overseeing HIV-related criminal cases for more just, less harmful outcomes for PLHIV facing HIV prosecution. Such materials can include databases, such as the HIV JUSTICE Toolkit, with case law and judgments, examples of good legislation and bills, prosecutorial guidelines, and other guidance on reducing the harms of HIV criminalization and ensuring PLHIV experience fair and due process of the law. Prosecutorial guidelines should specify which acts may warrant application of the law and those that do not, and provide evidence-based recommendations regarding HIV risk, the nature of HIV as a chronic manageable condition, mental culpability, evidence required and defenses in relation to HIV-related charges.
- Offer policy guidance, trainings and continuing education for police officers, community correction workers, lawyers, prosecutors and judges on the negative impact HIV criminalization has on public health, and HIV prevention, treatment and care issues so that misconceptions about the virus and how it is transmitted can be eliminated. This can lead to better outcomes in arrests and how cases are tried while reducing the inappropriate use of criminal law and optimizing the chance that PLHIV who face charges will be treated fairly.
- Convictions of those who have been prosecuted for HIV-related crimes should be carefully reviewed by suitably trained individuals or panels with the power to order retrials, overturn convictions and/or grant pardons. Those convictions which do not meet key criminal law principles or reflect up-to-date science should be overturned and any accused serving time be immediately released from incarceration with pardons or similar actions to ensure that such charges do not remain on the person's records.
- Enact and maintain legal policies that protect the confidentiality of medical and counseling information. At the same time, PLHIV should have the right to protect their identity and privacy in HIV-related criminal proceedings. Courts can protect confidentiality through such measures as using pseudonyms, having closed hearings, and sealing court records.

3. *Meaningfully Involve People Living with HIV*

- Groups working to reform laws and policies should support and collaborate with PLHIV and intersecting criminalized populations (e.g., racial/ethnic minority groups, sex workers and people who use drugs) to work with governing bodies to advocate for HIV criminal law reform.
- Reform groups and HIV/human rights organizations should provide training and resources for PLHIV on legal issues, rights of PLHIV, advocacy efforts and support and legal services around HIV criminalization so they can better understand the law and advocate for themselves should they or their peers become victims of HIV criminalization as well as how to avoid HIV criminalization.
- Reform groups should involve PLHIV in efforts to reform laws and educational efforts, especially in leadership roles, as this can create positive contact with policy makers, the public and legal actors to dispel stereotypes and reduce stigma attached to living with HIV, as well as ensure changes in laws and associated policies reflects the lived experience of PLHIV.
- Healthcare providers should support and empower PLHIV to live dignified healthy lives, so that they learn the skills needed to negotiate safer sex practices and/or safely disclose their HIV status to prospective sex or needle-sharing partners if and/or when ready to do so. One way to do this is by connecting them to networks of PLHIV who have already learned such skills.

4. *Call for Increased Action by Policy Makers, Researchers, and Providers*

- Significantly expand access to and provision of successful HIV prevention, treatment and support programs which will create supportive rather than punitive environments. Such expansion ensures that all individuals have the ability to keep themselves HIV-free and, if living with HIV, are well supported and able to safely avoid transmitting HIV.
- Continue to build the research evidence about the public health and human rights harms of HIV criminalization and identify which evidence is most effective in persuading judges, parliamentarians, policy makers and the general public to improve legal environments.
- Provide trainings and educate providers on the legal environments they face when providing care for PLHIV. Such guidance can cover items such as how to maintain confidential records, what to do with search warrants, subpoenas and testifying in court against a client/

patient and clarify professional obligations regarding issues about HIV and the criminal law.

- High-level international bodies such as UNAIDS, UNDP and UNODC, as well as national government and policy-making bodies, should mobilize support for campaigns to repeal or reform harmful HIV criminal laws. Such high-level governing entities can also make public statements condemning HIV criminalization and point out that incarceration is one of the worst possible approaches in the HIV response and has no public health benefits.

- International agencies must ensure that existing policy guidance (e.g., UNAIDS/UNDP 2008 recommendations and UNAIDS 2013 guidance note) and other high-level recommendations (such as those of the Global Commission on HIV and the Law) are known to national and local governments and justice systems so that they are made aware of how best to avoid the overly broad use of the criminal law as a tool to address allegations of HIV non-disclosure, potential or perceived exposure and non-intentional transmission. In doing so, they should suggest alternatives to criminalization that are human-rights-based and grounded in best public health practices.

5.   *Counter Stigmatizing Media Reports and Increase Educational Campaigns*

- HIV agencies, public health entities and PLHIV can address sensationalized media coverage of HIV criminalization by educating reporters about the issue and about how coverage is stigmatizing and discriminatory and by encouraging them to provide more accurate and balanced reporting.

- Agencies and PLHIV can create films documenting the harms of HIV criminalization (e.g. *HIV is not a Crime*, *Positive Women: Exposing Injustice* and *More Harm than Good*) and make films open-access and widely available via social media, film events, and other showings as a way to educate others about the harms of HIV criminalization. Any funds that may be raised for such events can be donated towards grassroots efforts working on HIV criminalization reform.

- Develop media campaigns and share stories that are not being told in the media targeting potential complainants (e.g., people who do not have HIV or who do not know their status) and the general population that provide education about the harms of HIV criminalization.

- Support anti-stigma/criminalization and HIV/STD education campaigns designed for general populations, healthcare providers, criminal justice and law enforcement professionals, parliamentarians, and others as needed. Such campaigns should explain the current science of HIV transmission, prevention, and treatment, and the harms of HIV stigma and its relationship to criminalization.

In summary, the stigmatization of PLHIV remains our greatest challenge to the HIV response and there is no greater form of stigmatization then that which is legitimated by law, in this case HIV criminalization. The criminal law is a blunt tool and should be used sparingly. In the context of ongoing HIV-related stigma, the law's main utility is to ensure that people with HIV are protected from discrimination. HIV is a virus. PLHIV should not be subject to criminal punishment except in the rare case of proven malicious intent to transmit or expose others to HIV with the sole purpose to cause harm. There is a growing social global movement to address the punitive effects of the law, and numerous viable solutions, providing hope that we can end HIV criminalization, bringing us closer to dismantling stigma and curbing the HIV pandemic.

Resources

Bernard, E.J. (2007) Criminal HIV Transmission. NAM Publications @AIDSmap.com

Bernard, E.J. and Cameron, S. (2013) *Advancing HIV Justice: A Progress Report on Achievements and Challenges in Global Advocacy against HIV Criminalisation*. HIV Justice Network and The Global Network of People Living with HIV (GNP+). Brighton/Amsterdam.

Bernard, E.J. and Cameron, S. (2016) *Advancing HIV Justice 2: Building Momentum in Global Advocacy against HIV Criminalisation*. HIV Justice Network and The Global Network of People Living with HIV (GNP+). Brighton/Amsterdam.

Cameron, E. (2009) Criminalization of HIV Transmission: Poor Public Health Policy, *HIV/AIDS Policy and Law Review*, 14(2):1, 63-75.

Center for HIV Law and Policy Resource Bank. Retrieved December 17, 2017. (https://www.hivlawandpolicy.org/resources) The HIV Policy Resource Bank is a comprehensive database of quality materials on topics of importance to PLHIV, including HIV Criminalization, and their advocates.

Chen, A.J. (2016) HIV-Specific Criminal Law: A Global Review, *Intersect: The Stanford Journal of Science, Technology and Society*, 9(3): 1-22.

Csete, J. and Elliott, R. (2011) Criminalization of HIV Transmission and Exposure: In Search of Rights-Based Public Health Alternatives to Criminal Law, *Future Virology*, 6(8): 941–950.

Global Commission on HIV and the Law (2012) *Report: Risks, Rights and Health*, UNDP, HIV/AIDS Group, Bureau for Development Policy, New York. Retrieved December 19, 2017(https://hivlawcommission.org/report/)

HIV Justice Toolkit. Retrieved December 17, 2017 (http://toolkit.hivjusticeworldwide.org/) The HIV Justice Toolkit aims to support advocates, by providing a diverse array of research, advocacy, and policy resources from all over the world to oppose HIV criminalization at all levels—from educating communities and lawmakers to defending individual cases.

Mykhalovskiy, E. (2015) The Public Health Implications of HIV Criminalization: Past, Current, and Future Research Directions, *Critical Public Health*, 25(4): 373–385.

Stackpool-Moore, L. (2008) HIV-Verdict on a Virus: Public Health, Human Rights and Criminal Law. IPPF, GNP+ and ICW. Retrieved December 17, 2017(https://www.ippf.org/resource/verdict-virus-public-health-human-rights-and-criminal-law).

UNAIDS (2013) *Ending Overly Broad Criminalization of HIV Non-Disclosure, Exposure and Transmission: Critical Scientific, Medical and Legal Considerations*. Geneva. Retrieved December 17, 2017 (http://www.unaids.org/sites/default/files/media_asset/20130530_Guidance_Ending_Criminalisation_0.pdf).

UNAIDS and UNDP (2008) *Criminalization of HIV Transmission Policy Brief.* Geneva. Retrieved December 19, 2017 (http://www.unaids.org/en/resources/documents/2008/20081110_jc1601_policy_brief_criminalization_long_en.pdf).

SECTION II

Environmental Issues

Radiation Refugees and Chronic Exposure to Ionizing Radiation: The Rights of the Exposed

Majia Nadesan

The Problem

Radioactive zones have been described as "landscapes of risk" that are often represented by Hanford in the US, Ozersk in Russia, Chernobyl in the Ukraine, and Sellafield in the UK, but also include abandoned mining, refining, and military-industrial sites around the world. The number of sites is unknown because of lapses in record keeping and illicit dumping, but one review of US Department of Energy documents by *The Wall Street Journal* identified 517 sites in the US alone considered for radioactive clean-up by a special government remedial action program. Radioactive landscapes of risk are hazardous because they are contaminated with higher-than-ordinary electromagnetic radiation (such as gamma rays and X-rays) and the radioactive elements that are the source of these emissions. Uranium, Strontium-89, Cesium-137, and Cobalt-60 illustrate a few of the radioactive elements freed either by design or accident through the extraction, processing, and utilization of nuclear materials. These and other radionuclides pose special chemical and radioactive hazards to biological life as they are internalized and bioaccumulate in flora and fauna, as do other toxic non-radioactive elements, such as lead. For example, radioactive isotopes of strontium bioaccumulate in bones, teeth, and the brain as the body misidentifies this element as calcium.

Biological life evolved under electromagnetic radiation exposure, but efforts to determine "safe" levels of exposure for particular radioactive elements, some of which did not exist on earth prior to human engineering, are challenged by the contingencies of exposure and the particularities of the exposed, such as their age, sex, and general health. Uncertainties about radiation effects, particularly under conditions of chronic exposure, fundamentally complicate social justice for the exposed. Uncertainty adds to the procedural challenges associated with having voice in decision making regarding community exposure standards and legal recourse and compensation after contamination. For decades after World War II, legal recourse and compensation were denied to entire communities living in landscapes of risk after being exposed to atmospheric testing. For example, indigenous people exposed to atmospheric testing in the South Pacific Marshall Islands (1946–1955) were studied as experimental subjects by the US military, but to this day are still seeking full compensation for ongoing claims of acute health problems and property lost due to contamination. In 2012, Calin Georgescu, then United Nations Special Rapporteur on human rights and toxic waste, concluded after a visit to the Marshall Islands that many communities reported feeling like "nomads" in their own country. Although today special rapporteurs and more responsive legal systems enable airing of grievances, achieving full justice, including the restoration of environments and livelihoods, remains elusive. Moreover, polluters are now pushing for increasing allowable exposure levels in a global environment facing increased nuclear hazards.

Radioactive zones are likely to increase as problems of nuclear waste management lead to increased contamination from aging nuclear plants and industrial/medical operations, producing a new kind of environmental refugee and raising important questions about justice when exposure effects are protracted, potentially unfolding across generations. Aging nuclear infrastructures and climate change effects, such as more powerful hurricanes, are predicted to increase probability of major accidents, on the scale of the Chernobyl nuclear accident in the Ukraine in 1986 and the 2011 Fukushima Daiichi nuclear accident in Japan. Risk assessment research predicts a severe (Three Mile Island type) nuclear accident every 10–20 years, with a 50% chance of another Fukushima-scale accident or larger in the next 50 years, and a Chernobyl-scale event in the next 27 years.

The Fukushima Daiichi disaster illustrates the problem of rights in an environment of chronic, "low-level" radiation exposure. More than 150,000 people were evacuated in the wake of the March 11, 2011 nuclear crisis. Five years later, approximately 89,000 of these people remained unwilling to return home because of a new permissible exposure level set by the national government at a level 20 times higher for citizens than prior to the disaster. In 2017, the Japanese government ended subsidies for "voluntary evacuees," incentivizing them to return to homes officially de-contaminated to the new level, but whose communities face constant re-contamination by mountain watersheds that slough radioactive elements in heavy rains. Fukushima's refugees have lost the right to an environment free from increased radiation hazard. UN Special Rapporteur Anand Grover concluded from his November 2012 visit to Japan that more should be done to protect and assist affected citizens. He also expressed concerns about the crisis management during the disaster and the subsequent response policies by the government and Tepco, the private utility owning and operating the Daiichi plant. Warning of the dangers of radioactive particles in food and water, he urged the Japanese government to incorporate citizen radiation findings in decision making about decontamination and exclusion zones and he promoted the participation of communities in the health decisions affecting them.

Japan is not alone in facing social justice issues around radiation contamination. As noted above, problems of chronic exposure and radiation refugees can be traced back to the World War II bombings in New Mexico in the US and Nagasaki and Hiroshima in Japan. Radiation refugees were produced during the Cold War period of atmospheric testing in the Bikini Atoll, Australia, and in the Southern Urals by nuclear weapons and their facilities. Many more people simply remained in environments contaminated by nuclear production and technologies, as illustrated by the "downwinders" living in the American Southwest. The stories of those living in risk landscapes are rarely disseminated widely, for many complex reasons, but significant among them is the tendency for exposed populations to be poor, rural, and often indigenous.

As is the case with other environmental hazards, indigenous and poor people in rural areas are often overrepresented among chronically exposed people. For example, in the US, the Tewa and Navajo people have lived for decades in an environment contaminated by uranium mining initiated during World War II. Uranium freed up by mining circulates in local air, soil, and water, presenting chronic exposure risks. Traditional food sources for indigenous people, such as the Navajo, often bear disproportionately more contaminants. Indigenous people living in the Arctic region face radioactive food hazards assessed at five times the level found in temperate regions. The complex pathways whereby radionuclides, such as radiocesium and uranium, bioaccumulate in living beings and causes disease are not fully understood and few studies have addressed how internal radionuclides interact with other environmental pollutants. Yet, research has established that indigenous people have higher cancer rates than other groups, among other environmentally mediated diseases.

Researchers at the University of Mexico investigating uranium effects among native Southwest people have found links between exposure and cardiovascular disease, dysfunction in the immune system, and a general increase in autoimmune disease among older exposed individuals. Radiation's landscapes of risk are scattered across the globe with increasing probability of escalating in number as aging nuclear infrastructures and climate change processes increase accidents. Social justice issues raised by exposure to radiation include violation of the exposed population's natural rights to life and cultured living. Social justice issues also derive from the inequitable distribution of societal risk produced by radiation contamination. Finally, barriers to full procedural rights for the exposed raise social justice issues that have been officially acknowledged by special rights rapporteurs, yet never fully resolved. These social justice issues will become increasingly relevant as environments become increasingly contaminated.

Research Evidence/State Of Knowledge About Problem

The scope of the problems of the exposed, including numbers impacted and full range of effects, have yet to be fully mapped. Part of the problem in mapping the scope of effects is that no scientific consensus exists on how increased levels of radioactive contamination affect biological life in complex systems. Scientific studies on specific human populations, such as those derived from the Atomic Bomb Casualty Commission and the Japanese Radiation Effects Research Foundation (RERF) have revealed adverse long-term effects. In 2012, the REFR reported finding no threshold below which radiation doses are harmless and linked exposure with circulatory, respiratory, and digestive disease, in addition to cancer and leukemia, with effects documented at exposure levels of 20 millisieverts, noting an upward curvature of effects for low doses. Studies on exposed animal populations, such as those found in Chernobyl, have documented reduced fertility and smaller heads and brains in offspring. It remains an open question whether and how effects detected in exposed animal populations living in high-risk landscapes are replicated in human populations.

The "linear no-threshold" model of ionizing radiation exposure effects posits no threshold of safe exposure. Although this model has been widely adopted, including by the International Atomic Energy Agency (IAEA), in practice most nations set a *permissible dose* standard that is typically set as low as reasonably achievable. The allowable dose is usually arrived at through risk assessments that incorporate scientific data on exposure effects and cost–benefit analysis. However, there exists considerable scientific disagreement concerning basic assumptions about exposure effects and acceptable levels of risk. As noted by Timothy Jorgensen, Associate Professor of Radiation Medicine, Georgetown University, "safe" has a fluid meaning and ultimately refers to an "acceptable level of risk," a level which produces considerable disagreement. Conceptualization, measurement, and administration of the permissible dose are fraught with controversy. Moreover, the risks from radiation exposure are not born equally across the population as the youngest among us have the greatest biological vulnerability. The 2006 US National Academies' panel on the risks of low-level radiation, the Biological Effects of Ionizing Radiation (BEIR) VII report, found that overall fatal cancer risk for females was 37.5% greater than for males exposed to the same radiation dose, and children are even more vulnerable. Moreover, radiation exposure presents special hazards of risk transferability as genetic and epigenetic damage resulting from exposure can be transmitted and amplified across generations, a process documented as early as the 1930s by geneticists studying X-rays and radium exposure effects on animal populations, but also documented in highly exposed Chernobyl clean-up liquidators. More research is needed to understand the scope, contingencies, and significance of problems of the exposed, particularly with respect to their rights when confronted with chronic exposure to elevated levels of radionuclides in air, food, and water.

Uncertainties regarding radiation effects will continue to complicate victims' efforts at redress. However, although disagreement exists over biological effects, there is widespread consensus that people living in irradiated landscapes of risk suffer greater psychological depression and loneliness, conditions exacerbated by devastated livelihoods and fractured communities. Masao Tomonaga, director emeritus of the Japanese Red Cross Nagasaki Atomic Bomb Hospital, describes lifelong fear and anxiety afflicting the radiation-exposed in Japan, the *hibakusha*: "The anxiety they still feel regarding potential aftereffects emerging in their own bodies or genetic effects in their offspring is quite beyond imagination ... An instantaneous exposure in August 1945 has kept survivors imprisoned by aftereffects for 70 years." Moreover, those individuals coded as exposed are often doubly victimized through symbolic stigmatization. Robert Jacobs of the Hiroshima Peace Institute warns that radiation has the capacity to make people "invisible," stripping them of the right to be recognized fully.

The case examples provided by the Chernobyl and Fukushima disasters demonstrates that governments are likely to increase radiation exposure levels after radiological releases. Most recently, there has been a global trend to increase allowable exposure levels in anticipation of future accidents. For example, the US Environmental Protection Agency released new guidance on radiological emergencies that increases by tenfold and more the acceptable threshold of radionuclides in water for a protracted period of a year. These examples illustrate a tendency for governments to increase allowable radiation exposure levels in the wake of increased contamination.

The costs and challenges of radioactive decontamination evidenced by the Chernobyl and Fukushima accidents, combined with the uncertainties associated with exposure, have prompted some organizations, including the Organisation for Economic Co-operation and Development, to recommend a gestalt shift from evacuations to adaptation, a practice that is being encouraged by the Japanese government as it lifts mandatory evacuation orders and encourages residents to return to areas with still-elevated external radiation levels. However, encouraging people to live in environments admittedly contaminated raises significant legal and ethical questions, including the transformation of people into test subjects. This transformation is particularly concerning given the types of effects found by researchers studying the transgenerational effects of animals living under conditions of chronic low-level exposure to radionuclides. The idea that the way to respond to radiation emergencies is through adaptation ultimately shifts the locus of risk to exposed communities.

Recommendations and Solutions

There are three important recommendations that can be drawn from this analysis of social problems of radiation exposure.

- Identify and reduce hazards across the vast apparatuses that produce radioactive contamination
- Explicit expansion of the ethics of radiation protection to include Aarhus Convention principles of environmental justice: access, participation, and procedural justice
- More accountable research identifying, mapping, and studying radiation risks in contaminated zones by researchers free of conflicts of interest

1. Identifying and Reducing Radiation Hazards Across Supply and Utilization Chains.

Radioactive contamination is produced across many supply chains, ranging in application and across industries. Radioactive waste is produced in mining and fracking, in the processing of rare earths for electronics and uranium for nuclear energy, in military research and weapons development, and in nuclear medicine. Prevention of accidents and long-term storage of nuclear waste are ongoing challenges that have not been appropriately tackled because of institutional reluctance to prioritize these agendas. For example, challenges arising from radioactive remediation and long-term waste storage have encouraged nuclear plant operators and regulators to extend the lifespans of aging nuclear energy infrastructures, rather than decommission reactors. Many aging reactors are located in close proximity to major metropolitan areas. The prioritization of short-term economic gain by powerful corporate and governmental actors under this scenario amplifies long-term risks to human and environmental health, especially under conditions of climatic change. There must be renewed commitments to, and accountability for, the problems of aging nuclear infrastructures, radioactive waste, and newly developed small-scale nuclear weapons. Increased public awareness and procedural justice can help increase polluter and governmental accountability.

2. Expansion of ethics of radiation protection.

The United Nations Economic Commission for Europe (UNECE) Convention on Access to Information, Public Participation in Decision-Making and Access to Justice in Environmental Matters adopted on June 25, 1998 (entered into force on October 30, 2001) offers one model for increasing institutional accountability. Known as The Aarhus Convention, this convention articulates a set of procedural rights for environmental justice, including the rights to access to environmental information, to participation in environmental decision-making procedures, and to procedural justice, grounded in "the right to review procedures to challenge public decisions that have been made without respecting the two aforementioned rights or environmental law in general." The right to access to information is foundational for meaningful participation in environmental decision-making procedures. The Aarhus Convention has not been widely adopted outside of the European Union.

More efforts are needed to make environmental information accessible. The UN 1972 Stockholm Conference on the Human Environment instituted this goal with the Earthwatch system, aimed at systematic and global environmental monitoring. Earthwatch includes the Global Environment Monitoring System (GEMS) program and INFOTERRA, the Global Environmental Exchange Network, charged by The United Nation Environmental Programme (UNEP). The INFOTERRA system operates through a network of affiliated national centers and offers a range of environmental information products and services (including environmental bibliographies; directories of sources of information; query–response services; environmental awareness leaflets). However, governments vary considerably in their reporting standards and practices. More critically, the Earthwatch system, and INFOTERRA in particular, are not easily accessed on the internet and cannot be readily navigated when found. Public access to environmental-information systems should be guaranteed and enabled, both technologically and in terms of the intelligibility of information, especially in the wake of radioactive contamination. One immediate step would entail enabling public access to atmospheric radioactivity data generated by the Comprehensive Nuclear-Test-Ban Treaty's verification regime

Information access should not end with respect to environmental monitoring data. Exposed populations must also have access to information and decision making regarding known and suspected risks in language they can understand. Data needed for an informed risk assessment would include levels and forms of exposure, as well as known and suspected short- and long-term biological effects. Debates about effects should be included so that communities can adjudicate acceptable risk.

Those individuals subjected to increased exposure levels must have procedural justice. The question of who decides what is safe is a critical one, as is the question of an appropriate response. Social-rights proponents and conventions such as Aarhus argue that exposed populations must have the right to participate fully in this process. Moreover, procedural justice processes must not homogenize impacted populations. The Fukushima Daiichi radiation refugees are mostly women with children. Older populations in Japan have been more willing to assume the risks of increased exposure, either remaining in, or returning to, zones with elevated radiation levels. Justice must be tailored appropriately to the special vulnerabilities and needs of particular populations.

3.   More accountable research on radiation exposure in real-world conditions.
More studies are needed by researchers free of conflicts of interest, aimed at assessing long-term risks under real-world exposure

conditions. This research should address how radionuclides circulate through environments and biological life forms and map their interactions with other forms of contamination, such as non-radioactive but toxic substances, ranging from elements such as lead to industrial and agricultural chemicals. Research conducted on exposed human populations must attend carefully to vulnerable populations and expand ethical accountability, well beyond the lax standards of the past. Research should include the voices of those studied and researchers must be responsive to their needs. Deployment of non-traditional, subject-centered methodologies, such as voluntary self-reported health surveys, can increase stakeholder voice in research protocols and supplement strictly empirical forms of data collection that discount the experiences of the exposed. The results of research effects studies must also be made publicly available in forms that are accessible and intelligible to general audiences.

The problems of radiation contamination need to be prioritized and solutions implemented because unmitigated contamination poses a significant discounting of humanity's future. Indeed, perhaps the greatest tragedy of elevated exposure is that catastrophic effects, such as increased mortality and reproductive problems, tend to be protracted across time, thereby impeding efforts to quantify and prioritize radiation risk. As the planet becomes more contaminated, the long-term effects from chronically elevated exposure will become more evident, but the time for remediation will have elapsed. Change is needed now. The recommendations detailed here provide a template for action.

Key Resources

Barker, H. and Johnston, B. (2000) Seeking Compensation for Radiation Survivors in the Marshall Islands, *Cultural Survival Quarterly Magazine*. Available https://www.culturalsurvival.org/publications/cultural-survival-quarterly/seeking-compensation-radiation-survivors-marshall-islands

Blowers, A. (2017) Nuclear's Wastelands part 1—Landscapes of the Legacy of Nuclear Power, *Town & Country*, April, 303-308.

European Commission (2017, February 3 last update) Environment: The Aarhus Convention. Available http://ec.europa.eu/environment/aarhus/ accessed December 6, 2017.

Gakkai, S. (2017) September 14. Eliminating the Nuclear Threat. *The Japan Times*. Available https://www.japantimes.co.jp/news/2017/09/14/national/eliminating-nuclear-threat/#.WeTbKDvdnwk accessed September 15, 2017.

Grover, A. (2012) November 26. "UN Special Rapporteur on the Right of Everyone to the Enjoyment of the Highest Attainable Standard of Physical and Mental Health, Country Visit to Japan, 15 to 26 November 2012." United Nations Human Rights: Office of the High Commissioner. Available http://www.ohchr.org/_layouts/15/WopiFrame.aspx?sourcedoc=/Documents/HRBodies/HRCouncil/RegularSession/Session23/A-HRC-23-41-Add3_en.pdf&action=default&DefaultItemOpen=1 accessed December 27, 2017.

Jacobs, R. (2014) The Radiation that Makes People Invisible: A Global Hibakusha perspective, *The Asia Pacific Journal*, 12(31.1): 1-11.

Jorgensen, T.J. (2017) Fukushima and Acceptable Risk, *The Conversation*. Available https://theconversation.com/acceptable-risk-is-a-better-way-to-think-about-radiation-exposure-in-fukushima-56190

Kyne, D and Bolin, B. (2016) Emerging Environmental Justice Issues in Nuclear Power and Radioactive Contamination, *International Journal of Environmental Research and Public Health*, 13: 1-19

Møller, A., Bonisoli-Alquati, A., Rudolfsen, G. and Mousseau, T. (2011) Chernobyl Birds Have Smaller Brains, *PlOS One*, 6(2): e16862.

Nuclear Energy Agency of the Organization for Economic Co-Operation and Development (2016) Management of Radioactive Waste after a Nuclear Power Plant Accident NEA No. 7305.

Ozasa, K. et al (2012) Studies of the Mortality of Atomic Bomb Survivors. Report 14, 1950–2003: An Overview of Cancer and Noncancer Diseases, *Radiation Research*, 177: 229-243.

Singer-Vine, J., Emshwiller, J., Parmar, N. and Scott, C. (2018) Waste Land: America's Forgotten Nuclear Legacy, *The Wall Street Journal*. Available http://projects.wsj.com/waste-lands/ accessed February 14, 2018.

UN Expert Warns of Situation Faced by Marshall Islands Citizens Affected by Nuclear Tests (2012) March 30. UN News Centre. Available http://www.un.org/apps/news/story.asp?NewsID=41677#.U9gRaPldXwA-- accessed December 8, 2017.

Wheatley, S., Sovacool, B. and Sornette, D. (2015) Of Disasters and Dragon Kings: A Statistical Analysis of Nuclear Power Incidents & Accidents, *Physics and Society*, 14: 1-24.

SIX

The Effects of "Natural" Disasters on Older Adults in South Asia: The Case of Intersectional Identities

Tirth Bhatta, University of Nevada, Las Vegas
Moushumi Roy, Michigan State University
Nirmala Lekhak, University of Nevada, Las Vegas

The Problem

This chapter offers a critique of the homogenization of older adults in research, discusses its implications for disaster research, and offers policy recommendations. Older adults have been mostly understood as experiencing health and well-being evenly. Hence, older populations are often considered a homogeneous group based on their health outcomes. The underlying assumption of homogeneity among older adults in terms of health outcomes (i.e., assumption that aging inevitably leads to poor health) has resulted in their classification as a vulnerable group. However, this type of categorization is problematic because older adults vary in educational attainment, health status, income, and wealth. Given these variations, the socioeconomic resources and services needed to cope with the adverse effects of natural disasters may differ between the groups of older adults. In this regard, we currently need to focus on policy changes to better assist older adults in South Asia who are more likely to bear the brunt of natural disasters.

Natural disasters have had devastating consequences, particularly, for people living in Asia. Between 1970 and 2014, natural disasters related deaths surpassed 2 million, constituting 56.6% deaths globally. During the same period, 87.6% of people (i.e., 6 billion people) affected globally resided in Asia and Pacific region. Recent evidence regarding natural disasters continues to make Asia-Pacific the world's most disaster-prone region. This part of the world experienced 160 calamities in 2015, which constituted 47% of the world's catastrophes. In 2016, seven of the top ten countries for the number of natural disasters were in Asia.

The mainstream understanding of natural disasters that tends to consider them as unavoidable and universal in terms of their devastating consequences, often fails to recognize heterogeneities in a population. The intersectional identities of older adults as defined by caste, race, class, gender, religious background, and sexuality constitute heterogeneity in various outcomes such as economic status, health, and functioning. Those identities serve as "interlocking system of oppression" and are "part of one overarching structure of domination." The acknowledgment of heterogeneities due to intersectional identities of older adults requires us to interrogate uneven impacts of natural disasters on older adults. Scholars, as well as policy makers, need to recognize that the differential experiences of older adults in an event of a natural disaster are due to their structural location. For instance, in order to understand why older adults from lower castes experience higher impacts of natural disasters, yet receive less post-disaster support from governmental agencies, it is necessary to consider the structural location associated with their intersecting identities. Such allowance is critical to forging public consensus for policies to adequately address heterogeneous impacts of natural disasters on older adults.

The process of developing a comprehensive understanding of the origins of natural disasters and its consequences for older adults begins by challenging the mainstream assumption that allows us to analyze such issues only through a decontextualized and depoliticized lens. Future scholarship in South Asia needs to shed light on the social, political, and economic forces that endanger socially vulnerable groups (e.g., poor lower-caste older adults) by forcing them to bear the brunt of various natural disasters such as earthquake, landslide, flood, drought, and heatwave. We also need to guard against attempts to ignore or trivialize the unnatural consequences of disasters even when they may be "natural" in origin. The overemphasis on the naturalness of disasters absolves people in power from owning responsibility to redress the disproportionate adverse effects of disasters on socially marginalized groups.

Research Evidence

Guha-Sapir defines natural disasters as "a situation or event that overwhelms local capacity, necessitating a request at the national or international level for external assistance; an unforeseen and often sudden event that causes great damage, destruction and human suffering" and leads to devastating consequences for people living in South Asia. With 52 disasters and 14,647 deaths, South Asia accounted for 64% of the total global deaths due to natural disasters in 2015. Consequently, South Asia is deemed as one of the most vulnerable sub-regions in Asia to experience natural disasters. The frequency of such disasters and death has continued unabated. Very recent floods in India and Bangladesh took away lives of 1,200 people and destroyed 950,000 houses impacting 41 million people. Similarly, 143 people lost lives and more than 460,000 were displaced from their homes. Along with floods, heatwaves and droughts have become common occurrences with tragic consequences for people living in South Asian countries like India, Pakistan, and Nepal.

Countries in South Asia are also expected to experience a substantial increase in their population in upcoming decades. Population projections indicate that total population (currently 1.6 billion) could cross over 2.2 billion by 2050. Comprising 6.3% in 2000, older populations (i.e., 60 years and above) are expected to comprise 19% of total population in South Asia by 2050. The consistent increase in the population size among the elderly in South Asia further complicates the existing risks of natural disasters in this region. For instance, most of the countries in South Asia lack adequate public infrastructures to deliver early warnings of natural disasters. Advance notifications can facilitate prompt evacuation and relocation to safe places. Lack of such resources poses significant risks of serious injury or death for older adults. Even in the countries with a well-developed warning and evacuation systems, older people faced more challenges. In the United States, 75% of people the worst hit or killed by Hurricane Katrina were 60 years and older. Additional risks posed by declining physical and cognitive health in later years have been offered as the explanation for disaster-related higher mortality among older adults. For example, 56% of those who lost their lives in earthquake and Tsunami in Asia in 2011 were 65 years and older.

Evidence regarding disproportionate impacts of natural disasters on older adults has led scholars to categorize them as a vulnerable population group. The vulnerability is defined by Wisner and colleagues as "the characteristics of a person or group and their situation that influence their capacity to anticipate, cope with, resist, and recover from the impact of a natural hazard." Categorization of certain social groups as more vulnerable than others has implicitly challenged historic conceptualization of disasters as "natural" and supreme, and as "acts of God." It has recognized that people's circumstances modify the impacts of natural disasters on their lives. Similarly, studies conducted in Western nations have documented higher mortality among older adults in combination with poor health and well-being outcomes among the survivors. Interpreted as the post-disaster growth, some studies have also documented increased resiliency, religiosity, and spirituality among older adults who have undergone traumatic experiences of natural disasters.

Prior scholarship also considers women, racial minorities, and individuals living in poverty as vulnerable groups. These populations have been found to experience negative post-disaster outcomes such as death, disability, and depression than their counterparts. Although addressing population group differences in post-disaster outcomes, this line of research has rarely examined the role of systemic forces (e.g., policies, laws) that is socio-political in nature and contributes to the formation of vulnerability among certain social groups (e.g., lower-caste poor older women). Overlooking the intersecting influences of multiple identities determined by caste, class, gender, sexuality, and age in the post-disaster situation, studies have implicitly positioned these social groups as independent and homogeneous.

Another line of inquiry sheds light on social and political forces that "normalize the injustices of race and class" by "depoliticizing the calamity." Consequently, this scholarship provides a vigorous critique of the mainstream tendency to present a natural disaster as an "equal opportunity killer." This research exposes "ecologically destructive practices by political and economic forces, like degrading forests, engineering rivers, filling in wetlands, and destabilizing the climate" as being responsible for magnifying the destructive effects of a disaster. A large number of people living in metropolises/urban slums in South Asia find themselves living in close proximity to the flood-prone areas. Due to unstable low-wage employment and lack of public housing, poor and working-class people are forced to live in low-lying areas prone to more flooding. It is estimated that 4 million people live in slums in Dhaka and more than 6 million people are slum dwellers in Mumbai. Living in these slum quarters increases their susceptibility to death during a natural disaster.

Experiences of these structural disadvantages that has already crippled their lives get compounded by disasters. Structural location of race and class also determines a group's ability to receive emergency responses in a timely manner. For instance, African American communities in the U.S. tend to receive less priority in evacuation and relocation than White communities. African Americans in general, but particularly poor, are also likely to face difficulties obtaining loans and finding temporary and permanent housing. Even the media coverage of natural disasters tends to differ, when the impacted are racial minorities. Oftentimes, sporadic individual acts of stealing are used to demonize the whole community, effectively fueling public opposition to the disaster relief.

Spearheaded by environmental justice scholars, this line of scholarship has been central in establishing the role of social inequalities in increasing the vulnerability of various social groups to disasters, which in turn affects "their ability to respond and bounce back." Theoretical orientation underlying recent research endeavors have begun to recognize the significance of an intersectionality framework. These endeavors, often focused on race, class, and gender dynamics, however, have paid very little scholarly attention to intersections with age. This is especially apparent in scholarship on the impacts of natural disasters in South Asia. Existing research in South Asia, relying on the vulnerability paradigm, has documented disproportionate impacts of disasters on poor, women, and older adults. These studies have enhanced our understanding of disadvantages along binary social identity (e.g., men and women). However, there has been very little attempt to theorize intersecting influences along multiple social identities (e.g., caste, class, gender, religion, sexuality, and age).

Recommendations and Solutions

In this chapter, we critically explored the existing arguments emphasizing how the assumption of homogeneity among older adults shapes policy responses to natural disasters. We offer the following policy recommendations to develop scholarship and social support mechanisms that are cognizant of intersecting identities of older adults. Finally, we see the need for social movement–oriented approaches that can tackle deep-rooted structural inequities that keep older adults disadvantaged in the first place.

1) *More research on natural disasters and impact on diverse older populations*: Future scholarship analyzing effects of natural disasters on older adults in South Asia should seriously consider the intersection of multiple social identities of older adults. This way studies will help us understand the structural roots of heterogeneous economic and health outcomes among older adults during the pre-disaster period. Additionally, intersectionality would provide us with a nuanced understanding

of how the catastrophic effects of natural disasters might exacerbate existing inequities. More research on intersectionality will inform public and in turn, will raise awareness in support of policies which will be better equipped with rectifying the system of oppression that exists in South Asian countries. A lack of awareness of the role of societal factors in contributing to the disadvantaged status of older adults may be behind the limited interest in old age policies to help socially and economically disadvantaged older adults. Several countries in South Asia lack social security and Medicare equivalent health care systems to support their older citizens. It is commonly understood that in the South Asian countries, regardless of household socio-economic status, families are expected to provide all material support (e.g., to pay for health care) to their older parents. This problematic assumption absolves the state's responsibility to provide insurance or social security benefits to disadvantaged older members of the society.

2) *Immediate Emergency Relief—Immediate needs for shelter, infrastructure, and food:* While developing policies to reduce the impacts of natural disasters for the disadvantaged in South Asian societies, policy makers must consider both the praxis and the policy. It is critical to developing public infrastructures that serve the urgencies (e.g., food, shelter) of older adults those who are severely impacted by the disaster. Any decisions on how to provide for emergency needs should be carried out in close coordination with local community members. In their relief efforts, they should include members from disadvantaged caste, religion and minority groups.

3) *Trauma resources—More resources for psychological supports:* Additional resources need to be allocated to offer medical and psychological supports to socio-economically disadvantaged older adults. Availability of aids to support health and well-being will help them overcome disaster-related trauma including grieving for any loss of family members. Furthermore, we should also pay special attention to older adults living in rural areas. The lack of public health infrastructure in rural areas is likely to elevate the risk of natural disasters and to perpetuate later life health inequities. In addition, older adults should be provided with financial and housing support from federal government to rebuild and reconstruct their lives. Given that lower caste individuals do not receive equal access to emergency relief services (e.g., food and shelter) as their higher caste counterparts, the disaster relief efforts need to give special consideration to lower caste older adults including women.

4) *Long-term recovery support—Specific needs and policies:* Policy makers should focus on long-term policy changes that should include provisions for assisting disadvantaged older adults to prepare for and recover from the disaster. It should also focus on eradicating discriminatory legislations and policies that initiated the disadvantaged circumstances. Federal-level government institutions should coordinate with local partners to train older adults. The training should help them recognize early warning of natural disasters and develop self-care skills that they can use to remain safe and secure when disaster strikes. Policies should exclusively emphasize and implement coordinated actions between emergency management organizations, public health agencies, and medical providers to assist older adults with health needs. Older adults from oppressed groups, especially women should be included as active partners while formulating these policies.

5) *Social movement solidarity:* Social justice activists, environmental justice activists, and climate justice activists need to form a coalition to fight against social and economic policies that result in interconnected oppressive, exploitative, and natural disaster-inducing circumstances. Social justice movements in South Asia should also work towards forging a public consensus that recognizes the critical importance of public institutions for recovery and reconstruction. This will pressurize people in power to invest more resources in developing institutions to assist in relief efforts. An illustration of the importance of well-financed and transparent public institutions for reconstruction comes from Indonesia. After 2004 Tsunami in the province of Aceh, Indonesian government created Aceh Rehabilitation and Reconstruction agency, or Badan Rehabilitasi dan Rekonstruksi (BRR). This agency coordinated the efforts of governmental and non-governmental efforts with local agencies and operated transparently. The financial transparency was also incorporated within the agenda and action. Utilizing this agency Indonesia was successfully able to accomplish the task of reconstructing Aceh.

Similarly, despite possessing limited resources, Bangladesh has been able to build a robust early warning, public awareness, and evacuation system. The federal government has been successful in building community-level storm shelters in coastal regions, aided by early warning system. The local level volunteers play integral part in the spreading of cyclone-related warnings and in rescue operations. These measures have significantly reduced cyclone-related deaths. The Bangladesh model, is in some ways similar to the other models such as Cuba, which also depends on and engages local volunteers to warn and to evacuate people living in vulnerable areas. The systems such as the one developed by Bangladesh and Cuba is critical for poor older adults who may have additional health problems.

Key References

Bolin, B. and Kurtz. L.C. (2018) Race, Class, Ethnicity, and Disaster Vulnerability, in H. Rodriguez, W. Donnor, and J.E. Trainor (eds) *Handbook of Disaster Research* 2nd edn. *Handbooks of Sociology and Social Research*, New York: Springer, pp 181-203

Bullard, R.D. and Wright, B. (2012) *The Wrong Complexion for Protection: How the Government Response to Disaster Endangers African American Communities.* New York: NYU Press.

Cherry, K.E., Allen, P.D. and Galea, S. (2010) Older Adults and Natural Disasters: Lessons Learned from Hurricane Katrina and Rita, in P. Dass-Brailsford (ed) *Crisis and Disaster Counseling: Lessons Learned from Hurricane Katrina and Other Disasters*, Thousand Oaks, CA: Sage, pp 115-130.

Collins, P.H. (1990) *Black Feminist Thought: Knowledge, Consciousness, and the Politics of Empowerment.* Boston, MA: UnwinHyman.

Guha-Sapir D., Hoyois, P., Wallemacq, P. and Below, R. (2016) *Annual Disaster Statistical Review 2016: The Numbers and Trends.* Brussels, Belgium: Center for Research on Epidemiology of Disasters (CRED).

Katz, J.M. (2013) *The Big Truck that Went by: How the World Came to Save Haiti and Left behind a Disaster.* Macmillan.

Kim, SE., Li, H.M.D. and Nam, J. (2015) Overview of natural disasters and their impacts in Asia and the Pacific, 1970–2014, The Information and Communications Technology and Disaster Risk Reduction Division: UNESCAP.

Mohan, G. and Stokke, K. (2000) Participatory Development and Empowerment: The Dangers of Localism, *Third World Quarterly*, 21(2): 247-268.

Steinberg, T. (2006) *Acts of God: The Unnatural History of Natural Disaster in America* (2nd edn) New York: Oxford University Press.

Wisner, B., Blaikie, P., Cannon, T. and Davis, I. (2004) *At Risk: Natural Hazards, People's Vulnerability and Disasters* (2nd edn) New York: Taylor & Francis Group.

SEVEN

Energy Democracy: A Just Transition for Social, Economic, and Climate Justice

Todd E. Vachon, Sean Sweeney

The Problem

Humanity is facing a climate emergency. Ever-growing levels of fossil fuel use are stretching planetary limits by raising greenhouse gas (GHG) emissions and air pollution to dangerous levels. The current carbon-based energy system is negatively affecting the health and quality of life of the world's population and is disproportionately affecting marginalized populations, who have contributed the least to the problem. Record global temperatures and warmer ocean temperatures are increasing the odds of devastating hurricanes and extreme rain events in some locations and prolonged droughts and wildfires in others. According to UNICEF, unchecked climate change will deprive many millions of children access to the bare necessities of life—food, clean air, and water—and may lead to increased conflict, migration, and quite possibly the worst humanitarian crisis the world has seen.

Existing policies aimed at addressing climate change are primarily market-based, have not reduced global GHG emissions, and have often exacerbated existing social inequalities such as energy poverty (lack of access to energy services), racialized exposure to health risks, and decline of safe, secure, living-wage jobs. Support for such ineffective policies, or no policy at all, has been fueled in large part by the fossil fuel industry putting profits over planetary health and human well-being. Using their tremendous wealth and political influence, large corporations have blocked meaningful change by creating a false choice of "jobs versus the environment," and sowing doubt and climate denial among the public. At the same time, the world is experiencing record levels of economic inequality, with workers' rights and union representation under attack by many of the same corporations.

In what follows, we concisely summarize the research on climate change and mitigation efforts and then provide informed recommendations for social action and public policy solutions. Our focus is on the power generation sector as it represents the largest single contributor of GHG emissions globally and has been the sector most frequently targeted by public policy intended to reduce emissions. We argue that long-term strategies for a just transition to energy democracy are needed to address the interrelated, root causes of social, economic, and climate injustice. These strategies must be publicly driven and rooted in public ownership of the energy sector, if we are to have any realistic chance of avoiding very serious harms due to climate change.

Research Evidence

In 2017, the U.S. government's Global Change Research Program issued its Fourth National Assessment, reaffirming the established scientific consensus that: (1) global surface air temperature has increased by 1.0°C (1.8°F) since 1900; (2) sea levels have risen 8 inches in the same period; (3) our weather is already being impacted by the warming climate; and (4) the warming is caused primarily by human activity, particularly the combustion of fossil fuels such as oil, coal, and gas. Among the key contributors to warming, electric power generation is the single largest, accounting for 25% of total GHG emissions annually according to the Carbon Disclosure Project. According to the IEA, to keep global temperatures below the 2.0°C limit prescribed by climate scientists and enshrined in the Paris Climate Accord, energy-related GHG emissions would need to peak before 2020 and fall by more than 70% from today's levels by 2050. In other words, to prevent catastrophic climate change, a rapid and massive switch to renewable energy sources is required.

The past decade has seen the publication of several studies, such as the *Special Report on Renewable Energy Sources and Climate Change Mitigation* by the Intergovernmental Panel on Climate Change (IPCC) and the *Clean Energy Future* report by Synapse Energy Economics, which highlight the potential of renewable energy to meet most, if not all of the world's energy needs, within just a few decades, particularly if these are combined with a serious pursuit of efficiency gains and reasonable conservation measures. However, real commitments to renewable energy have proven politically difficult in the face of the entrenched lobbying power of the fossil fuel industry and the strong free-market ideology that influences economic policy making throughout the world. The Presidential election of Donald Trump, who has called climate change a "hoax," and the resulting industry capture of U.S. regulatory agencies such as the Environmental Protection Agency (EPA) and Department of Energy illustrates the magnitude of the challenges faced by those working to address climate change. For example, before assuming his role at the EPA, Trump's pick to lead the agency, Scott Pruitt, sued the EPA at least 14 times on behalf of fossil fuel companies trying to block environmental rules. The Sabin Center at Columbia Law School did an analysis of Trump appointees to environmental, energy, and natural resource agencies and found that 28% had close ties to the fossil fuel industry. According to a report in the *New York Times* in May 2017, Trump reversed course on 23 environmental rules and regulations during the first 100 days of his administration.

The most common efforts to reduce GHG emissions that are currently underway include various forms of carbon pricing (often taxation, but more frequently, emissions trading schemes). Unfortunately, these efforts have not been aggressive enough and have generally proven inadequate. According to the World Bank, only 13% of global GHGs are priced, and in more than 75% of cases, the price is less than $10 per ton—thus, far too low to drive any changes in investment behavior or production choices. For example, the most-developed carbon market in the world, the European Trading Scheme, had near zero impact on emissions levels in the EU during its first ten years. Some countries, such as Australia, adopted a carbon tax to reduce emissions at home (a tax that has since been repealed), but continued to extract and export massive amounts of coal to be burned in other parts of the world, such as China, Korea, and Japan. Private investment in renewable energy sources has also been insufficient in terms of meeting climate targets. According to the IEA, all renewable energy sources combined generated just 22% of global electricity at the end of 2013. In July 2017, the IEA noted that, over the past five years, new wind and solar installations globally had been almost entirely offset by the slowdown in nuclear and hydropower investments, which declined by over half over the same period. In other words, renewables have done almost nothing in terms of displacing the use of fossil fuels in power generation.

Current market-based solutions also reinforce or often exacerbate existing social and economic inequalities. Despite more energy being generated every year, 1.2 billion people still do not have regular access to electricity according to the IEA. Small island nations, which according to the IPCC have contributed less than 1% of total GHG emissions, are confronting the very real prospects of annihilation due to rising sea levels. Polluting fossil fuel plants are disproportionately located near marginalized communities while new green technologies, such as rooftop solar, are more likely to emerge in affluent areas. In sum, the privately owned, profit-driven energy system and concomitant market-based solutions to climate change have created an unequitable distribution of energy-related benefits and risks and are incapable of adequately reducing GHG emissions to the levels required to prevent serious harm to many millions from climate change.

Recommendations and Solutions

Energy Democracy

It has become increasingly clear that the transition to an equitable, sustainable economy can only occur if there is a break with profit-driven approaches and an embrace of public alternatives oriented toward the common good. The phrase "energy democracy" has emerged in recent years to represent a political, economic, and social project to simultaneously address climate change as well as social and economic injustice. The core tenet of energy democracy is the transfer of ownership and control of the energy sector to the public, which could be local communities, or to new and / or "reclaimed" old public entities such as utilities. The only way to ensure a just transition to renewable energy sources is to replace the profit motive as the primary factor in decision making regarding energy and replace it with the public interest. Publicly owned and democratically controlled energy systems whose guiding principal is maximizing the public good will not only facilitate the rapid transfer to renewable sources that is needed to address global climate change, but can also ensure that the transition is done equitably, protecting vulnerable workers and addressing existing environmental injustices. Energy democracy can take many forms, ranging from small-scale decentralized energy cooperatives to large state-owned entities—for some examples, see Kunze and Becker's *Energy Democracy in Europe: A Survey and Outlook*. Rather than advocating for any one particular model, we offer the following general recommendations for public policy and social action to move the dial toward energy democracy in order to address the interconnected problems of social, economic and climate justice.

Movement Building to Resist the Fossil Fuel Agenda

Achieving energy democracy requires building a broad-based and truly inclusive movement. A successful movement will be comprised of multiple constituencies, including environmentalists, labor groups, social justice organizations, and environmental and climate justice groups. The issues of social, economic, and climate justice are deeply interconnected and thus require overcoming entrenched divisions between various issue-based movements, and the formation of a broad consensus around energy democracy. Too often in the past, competing issue-based movements have found themselves engaged in fruitless inter-movement conflicts resulting in net losses for all. After all, the same corporations that are polluting the Earth are also exploiting workers, warming the climate, oppressing indigenous peoples, and reproducing other forms of discrimination and inequality.

To that end, climate activists must be cognizant of the impacts that mitigation plans may have on workers and marginalized communities. Workers must also recognize that fossil fuel use needs to be eliminated, but it must be done in a systematic way that does not place the burden on the backs of workers and low-income communities. These shared understandings can only arise through candid dialogue and engagement between various movements. Labor union members and leaders can begin by discussing the issue of climate change within their organizations. Likewise, environmental activists can bring the issues of employment and social justice into discussions at their organizations. Some examples of movement-building efforts currently underway include the Just Transition Alliance, the Labor Network for Sustainability, and Movement Generation in the U.S.; Indigenous Climate Action in Canada; and Trade Unions for Energy Democracy, an international effort.

Once organized, citizens must stand up to the power of the fossil fuel industry by engaging in a wide variety of forms of struggle and resistance at the local, state, and federal level. The time to decarbonize the economy is now and all legislative initiatives geared toward expanding fossil fuel extraction for either domestic use or export must be resisted. Projects such as the various tar sands oil pipelines in North America, and the expansion of coal power plants throughout Asia, have already faced organized resistance through letter writing, lobbying, demonstrating, and direct action. These efforts must be continued and expanded.

Just Transition Programs for Displaced Workers

While it's true that, on balance, environmental policies tend to create more jobs than they eliminate, this fact is of little comfort to the workers in fossil-fuel producing and using industries who are likely to lose their jobs as a result of climate protection policies, including coal miners, power-plant workers, and oil refinery workers. To protect these workers, a just transition program would include at minimum, a fund to provide financial support and opportunities for higher education for displaced workers and communities impacted by climate protection policies. These programs represent a direct challenge to the market-oriented approach to the economy by inserting democratic voice and state intervention to serve the interests of people before profits.

Not only should fossil fuel workers be protected because it is the right thing to do for them, but also because it is necessary to help build the broad-based support that is required for the implementation of strong climate protection measures. Without an adequate, just transition fund in place, displaced workers can and have rapidly become organized opponents to climate protection measures. Just transition plans and funds have been implemented to various degrees in several localities and at the state level in various parts of the world. Support is currently growing for national-level legislation in many countries.

Reverse Privatization of Energy Sector

The increasing privatization and corporate concentration of the energy sector over the past four decades has led to underinvestment, loss of jobs, reductions in wages and union coverage, worsening working conditions, and falling quality of service. Where privatizations have taken place, public control has normally been replaced by oligarchies. In the UK, six private corporations—just one of them British—dominate the power generation sector and, according to Enerdata, 57% of fuel used to generate electricity is imported. In the Philippines, the neoliberal Electric Power Industry Reform Act led to a 100% increase in power rates according to the Freedom from Debt Coalition and the Philippine Center for Investigative Journalism.

The resistance to privatization has been intense in numerous countries, such as Argentina, India, Indonesia, and Ghana. Protests have halted privatization proposals in Peru, Ecuador, and Paraguay. The fight for energy democracy can draw both knowledge and strength from the recent successes of the movement to protect and reclaim public services at the local, state, and national level. For a number of years, the Public Services International Research Unit (PSIRU) has documented struggles against privatization and forcefully made the case for reclaiming public services. Activists, scholars, and policy makers can make good use of PSIRU's studies and analyses to build public support for reversing privatization.

Take Back the City

According to the United Nation's *World's Cities in 2016* report, the majority of the world's population increasingly lives in cities, making the municipal level a key arena for action on climate change and energy democracy. The scale of the city is also ideal for building a publicly owned and managed energy system as it is close enough to local communities to remain democratically accountable. Movement-building has proved fruitful and effective in cities such as Berlin, New York, and London where solidarities have been formed between climate, labor, and social justice groups. With the rise of nationalist, right-wing parties at the national level in many countries, sub-state entities, such as cities, have become central sites of resistance and progressive alternatives. Resisting fossil fuels, reversing privatization by remunicipalizing utilities, and promoting energy democracy at the city level will build a base to create change at the national level.

Ballot Initiatives

Whether at the national, state, or local level, ballot initiatives are one way that energy democracy activists can bring the energy sector back into public hands. The rules about ballot initiatives vary greatly across political jurisdictions, but in places with a favorable legal climate, a concerted effort by activists can make a big difference. For example, in 2011, the residents of Boulder, Colorado voted in favor of cutting ties with the private utility company that had been contracted by the city and instead created its own, democratically accountable, public utility. In 2013, an alliance of more than 50 civic groups in Berlin, Germany pushed for a referendum on the remunicipalization of the distribution grid, and the creation of a democratic energy utility company. The campaign successfully collected the 200,000 petition signatures necessary to force the referendum and won the referendum vote with 83% majority. Unfortunately the initiative failed to reach the required voter quorum by just 21,000 votes because the local government moved the date of the referendum to a day that was different from the general election, thus undermining turnout. Regardless of being denied this victory, the campaign built enough public support and pressure to bring about the creation of a local grid operator and electricity supplier even if many demands, including greater public participation, remain unaddressed.

Public Investment in Renewables

Inadequate levels of investment in renewable energy are a major obstacle standing in the way of the transition to a sustainable energy system. Climate change mitigation as "an investment opportunity" has proven inadequate to address the problem of GHG emissions. Current market-oriented approaches to address this investment deficit, such as public–private partnerships and power purchase agreements, serve merely to place economic risk on the public while guaranteeing benefits to private investors. In assessing the rise in renewable energy over the past decade, a 2013 paper prepared for the OECD Round Table on Sustainable Development concluded that, "The most effective [policy] instruments [to spur growth in renewables] have been those that provide a predictable return to investors but shift the risk to rate payers or government budgets." Even so, these schemes are still not generating adequate levels of investment to meet the emissions reduction targets and are making renewable energy unnecessarily expensive and vulnerable to political backlash. In fact, the OECD's own *Business and Finance Outlook 2016* report stated that "the current designs of wholesale liberalized electricity markets are often not strategically aligned with the low-carbon transition." The two largest emitters of GHG emissions, by far, are China and the United States. China's power market is growing, the United States's is contracting, but both rely on private renewable energy with public subsidies in one form or another. Any country that successfully goes public can show that there is an alternative, hopefully leading others to follow.

The case for true public financing and ownership is compelling and may be the only way to overcome the investment deficit—likely the most significant impediment to the effort to decarbonize power generation. Further, the long-term financial benefits of public investment can be returned to the public in the form of energy cost savings. To achieve this end will require education, organization, and agitation. Policy makers must be informed that publicly financed and owned renewables are a win–win for taxpayers and the climate. Concerned citizens should start pushing for these investments now.

Key Resources

Brecher, J. (2016) *Climate Insurgency: A Strategy for Survival*. West Cornwall, CT: Stone Soup Books.

Fairchild, D. and Weinrub, A. (eds) (2017) *Energy Democracy: Advancing Equity in Clean Energy Solutions*. Washington, DC: Island Press.

Just Transition Centre (2017) *Just Transition: A Report for the OECD*. http://www.oecd.org/environment/cc/g20-climate/collapsecontents/Just-Transition-Centre-report-just-transition.pdf

Kishimoto, S. and Petitjean, O. (eds) (2017) *Reclaiming Public Services: How Cities and Citizens are Turning Back Privatisation*, Amsterdam: Transnational Institute.

Kunze, C. and Becker, S. (2014) *Energy Democracy in Europe: A Survey and Outlook*. Brussels: Rosa Luxemburg Stiftung.

Labor Network for Sustainability, 350.org, and Synapse Energy Economics (2016) The Clean Energy Future: Protecting the Climate, Creating Jobs, Saving Money. https://www.synapse-energy.com/sites/default/files/Clean-Energy-Future-15-054.pdf

Sweeney, S. (2012) Resist. Reclaim. Restructure: Unions and the Struggle for Energy Democracy, Foundational Document for *Trade Unions for Energy Democracy*. http://unionsforenergydemocracy.org/wp-content/uploads/2013/12/Resist-Reclaim-Restructure.pdf

Sweeney, S. and Treat. J. (2017) Preparing a Public Pathway: Confronting the Investment Crisis in Renewable Energy, Working Paper #10, *Trade Unions for Energy Democracy*. http://unionsforenergydemocracy.org/resources/tued-publications/tued-working-paper-10/

U.S. Global Change Research Program (2017) *Climate Change Impacts in the United States*. Fourth National Climate Assessment. http://www.globalchange.gov

Vachon, T.E. and Brecher, J. (2016) Are Union Members More or Less Likely To Be Environmentalists? Some Evidence from a National Survey, *Labor Studies Journal*, 41: 185-203.

Worldwatch Institute (2014) *State of the World 2014: Governing for Sustainability*. Washington, DC: Island Press.

SECTION III

Gender and Sexuality

EIGHT

Fostering Critical Awareness of Masculinity around the World

Kyle C. Ashlee, Leland G. Spencer, Michael Loeffelman,
Brandon Cash, and Glenn W. Muschert

The Problem

Fostering critical awareness of masculinity and gender inequality around the world is key to developing effective solutions to many social problems. Men in societies throughout the world enjoy privilege in the areas of power, wealth, and status. They are also responsible for a vast majority of acts related to gender violence and oppression around the globe. Yet, men's health disparities and changing economic patterns offer ever more complex constraints for what it means to be a man around the world.

Recognizing that research on masculinities often centers Western, white, heterosexual masculinities, it is important to consider how masculinities interact with nationality, culture, sexuality, gender identity, class, and other aspects of difference. Understanding masculinities intersectionally requires reflecting on the concepts of male dominance and toxic masculinity. Male dominance refers to the societal and cultural norms that favor men while marginalizing women, transgender people, and children. Toxic masculinity describes the harmful impacts of masculinities that emphasize dominance, the use of violence to solve problems, and the suppression of empathic emotions, like sadness, fear, and compassion. While the specifics of male dominance and toxic masculinity vary across time and cultures, many of these practices recur often enough for patterns to emerge.

Acknowledging the globally harmful aspects of male dominance and toxic masculinity is a point of entry to examine data about men's wellness, men's role in global violence, and the perpetuation of oppression around the world. A fundamental characteristic of toxic masculinity is what social psychology researchers describe as *the empathy gap*, or the decreased capacity of men to show concern for others.

Among men in many cultures, there are prescriptive norms for social behavior such as being a contender and winner, maintaining control of oneself and one's emotions, and being a provider and protector. As these norms are applied in practice, there develops a tendency for men and boys to sympathize less with the emotions, experiences, and values of others. Toxic masculinity also encourages men and boys to hide their own needs, challenges, and distress by shielding their authentic emotive experiences under a facade of dominance and aggression. This emotional suppression, coupled with male-dominated social environments, results in the diminishment of men's health and impedes men's relationships. Men are socialized to enact what Michael Kaufman calls a triad of violence—violence toward women, other men, and themselves.

The Research Evidence

Gender roles significantly affect physical and mental health. Globally, women face significant maternal health issues, are more likely than men to be victimized by domestic and sexual violence (usually perpetrated by men), and are more likely to suffer from mental illness and post-traumatic stress than men. Men, on the other hand, experience shorter life expectancy than women, are more likely to engage in substance abuse, to be a victim of homicide, and to die by suicide. Men use medical services at lower rates than women, possibly due to the norms of stoicism and self-reliance, which is a contributing factor to lower life expectancy. Collectively, data indicate that masculinity norms may contribute to health disparities for everyone.

Life Expectancy and Disease Burden

The World Health Organization (WHO) indicates that the average life expectancy at birth for the years 2000–2015 was 73.8 for females and 69.1 for males. The WHO also estimates key statistics for the Global Burden of Disease (GBD), which quantifies the health effects of over 100 diseases and injuries worldwide. In a 2010 study by the WHO, 56% of the total years of life lost around the globe to disease and injury were among men.

Mental Health, Substance Abuse, and Suicide

While WHO data estimate that women have a higher prevalence of mental illness and disorders, men greatly surpass women in substance abuse. For example, men are 2.5 times as likely to develop an alcohol dependency (20% lifetime dependency for men vs. 8% for women). Finally, GBD reports indicate that worldwide, men account for nearly two-thirds of deaths by suicide.

Homicide

With regard to crime and victimization, a study by the United Nations Office on Drugs and Crime reported a great gender disparity: 79% of homicide victims were men. However, even more striking is that 96% of homicide perpetrators worldwide are men, and among women 77% of those killed by homicide were killed by former or current romantic partners.

Domestic and Sexual Violence

Men's violence toward women is a major problem worldwide, and the WHO estimates that 30% of women have experienced sexual or physical violence by a partner. Women who experience intimate partner violence have more prenatal health problems, more exposure to sexually transmitted diseases, and are more at-risk for developing post-traumatic stress disorder or other mental health conditions. It is clear that toxic masculinity is harmful to men themselves as well as their families and intimate partners, in the form of health disparities and exposure to violence.

Recommendations and Solutions

To foster critical awareness of masculinities around the globe, individuals working within systems (e.g., political, social, legal, cultural) must acknowledge and initiate responses that lessen or eradicate the existence of male dominance. To address one aspect of institutionalized gender inequality, the framers of Rwanda's 2003 constitution included parliamentary gender quotas, giving the country the highest percentage of women in the legislature of any nation. In addition, coordinated efforts to challenge toxic masculinity need to counter cultural norms that celebrate harmful masculinity. Governments, schools, families, and communities can help boys and men cultivate empathy and compassion for others by teaching them the harmful effects of toxic masculinity.

The goals for fostering critical awareness of global masculinities must include identifying harmful behaviors associated with male dominance, recognizing aspects of culture that perpetuate toxic masculinity, and promoting healthy expressions of manhood. The authors' positionality as white male-identified United States citizens greatly influences their views on masculinity and gender. Thus, the following recommendations should be considered and modified according to the context and culture in which they are applied.

1. Assess and Revise Existing Policies Towards Gender Equality

Governmental policies and cultural practices simultaneously are influenced by, and shape social norms of masculinity. To break this cycle, policy makers and law makers should evaluate legislation, cultural customs, and representations in leadership which reinforce a culture of male dominance. An example of this type of assessment can be found in a 2006 report conducted by the European Union, which evaluates the impact of gender inequality in Finland's lawmaking and policy creation. Regional and national governments can then use their evidenced-based assessments to create committees, programs, and policies which establish gender equality in national decision making, as Norway did with the Gender Equity Council and Male Role Committee. A key aspect of tailoring effective solutions includes government-funded research to examine cultural attitudes about gender roles, masculinity, violence, familial roles, and household responsibilities. Results from national assessments and research should be shared publicly, similar to the 2015 YouGov global report on gender attitudes, which highlights the harmful effects of male dominance, as well as positive examples of gender equality in two dozen countries across the globe.

Legislators and policy makers should support the development of men's programs and centers, like Men for Change in South Africa or the Men's Center in Osaka, Japan, which provide culturally relevant support for men making positive changes through community engagement, men's health education, violence prevention, and fatherhood involvement. Advocacy groups can help legislatures understand the prominence of intimate partner violence, sexual assault, and rape, as crimes and as public health issues. Law makers may be more effective in establishing gender equality by developing policies which target the perpetrators of harm while supporting vulnerable populations. One example of this approach is the Swedish law which decriminalized prostitution and instead criminalizes the purchase of sex and human trafficking. Finally, legislation which provides at least 30 days of paid leave for all parents of newborn or adopted children, thus giving support for the development of strong families, has found success in many countries and can be implemented elsewhere.

2. Address Toxic Masculinity in Court Systems

Accountability for harmful behavior is a crucial aspect of raising awareness about masculinities around the world. Mechanisms for justice must support victims as well as perpetrators who have been conditioned by a culture which values men over women. In order to achieve this, judiciaries should educate judges about toxic masculinities and create specialized treatment court options for men who commit non-violent criminal offenses, similar to the Veterans Treatment Court focused on providing services to United States military veterans. Other specialized courts, including drug courts and mental health courts, have demonstrated an effective approach to addressing the root cause of criminal offenses for specific populations around the world, including in Australia, Canada, New Zealand, and the United Kingdom. These specialized courts are non-adversarial judicial programs, which provide treatment, counseling, academic and vocational training, housing, healthcare, and job placement services to help individuals in the criminal justice system lead healthier and more productive lives.

These programs might also include opportunities for men to discuss how male dominance and violence has negatively affected their lives, like the inmates of San Quentin Prison (California, USA) featured in the 2015 documentary, *The Mask You Live In*. Finally, law enforcement should be trained to intervene and help prevent men's violence against women, including sexual assault and domestic violence, through bystander intervention programs like Mentors in Violence Prevention and Men Can Stop Rape in the United States, or Partners for Prevention throughout Asia and the Pacific region.

3. Expand Educational Programs

Fostering critical awareness of masculinities must include expanding educational programs in schools around the world. Students must learn how a culture of male dominance harms everyone in society, including boys and men. Similar to the WizeGuys program out of Canada or the Healthy Boys Training conducted by Merge for Equality (Massachusetts, USA), educational programs should focus on developing respectful communication skills, identifying and expressing complex emotions, as well as the ability to show empathy and compassion for others. Additionally, schools can implement educational programs that explicitly address gender roles, consent, bullying, prevention, and intervention.

Training educators in diverse learning styles and gender bias is an important element of supporting gender equality throughout the educational curriculum, as outlined in the UNESCO Education 2030 Framework for Action. Teachers can implement strategies to address teacher and student gender bias, equal participation of boys and girls, gender neutral language, and fair discipline methods. Exposing boys and men to engaging feminist scholarship, like bell hooks' *The Will to Change* or Chimamanda Ngozi Adichie's *We Should All Be Feminists*, can help them see how everyone benefits from gender equality. Schools can create educational environments that allow boys and men to explore their gender identity with other boys and men, similar to *Maschile Plurale* (Plural Masculinities) in Italy, *Miessakit ry* (Men's Group Association) in Finland, and Humans United Strength Organization (HUSO) mentoring group in Hell's Kitchen, New York, USA. Finally, educators can use anonymous and private online chat rooms and blogs, like Masculinities 101, MasculinityU, Higher Unlearning, or The Good Men Project, to foster critical awareness of masculinities with students outside the classroom.

4. Engage Men in Their Communities

Community engagement is a powerful tool for creating social change, including raising awareness of masculinities around the world. Individuals need to reflect on what masculinity means in their community and interrogate the origin of those ideas, including culture, media, faith traditions, education, and industry. Existing community organizations, like women's advocacy groups or LGBTQ centers, might facilitate community dialogues on masculinity in order to develop male allies for their work or support men with marginalized identities. Community leaders can initiate public dialogue about issues related to masculinity and gender through marketing, social media, art, and scholarship. Messaging, like the Find Your Magic campaign spearheaded by Lynx in the UK, or #blackboyjoy championed by Chance the Rapper in the United States, should focus on challenging toxic behaviors of masculinity, modeling positive examples of healthy masculinity, and illustrating how male dominance is harmful to everyone in society. Additionally, community organizers looking to engage men in efforts for gender equality can leverage already existing global movements, including Oxfam's We Can End Violence Against

Women program happening in Pakistan, the White Ribbon Campaign out of Canada, or the United Nations' HeForShe campaign.

5. Involve Men in Family Life

Awareness of masculinities can also be expanded by actively involving men in family life. Engaged parents and guardians can have a profound impact on the way a child thinks about masculinity and gender equality. Parents should facilitate informed conversations about gender, healthy sexuality, consent, and violence prevention with children and other family members. Parents can encourage boys to express their gender identity genuinely, beginning at a young age. Parents may choose to expose their children to positive examples of masculinity and gender equality in toys, books, and movies. Fathers and male role models need to exhibit healthy expressions of masculinity while also facilitating healthy rites of passage into adulthood, such as those performed at the Australian and New Zealand Men's Leadership Gathering through a program called Pathways to Manhood. Here, teenage boys and their fathers congregate in the Australian wilderness, where the boys are publicly acknowledged as men in a supportive and empowering environment.

Active parenting also has the potential to transform men, allowing them to love and support another person openly. A 2011 UN report, *Men in Families*, highlights the many positive benefits that have resulted from men becoming more involved in family life around the world.

Positive outcomes for gender equality are found in countries where more men play an active role in raising children, providing physical and emotional support to their children and family members. Specifically, the equal sharing of household responsibilities results in increased reproductive health, more effective family planning, improved maternal and newborn health, as well as social and educational benefits for children. Men can also be involved with family life by providing guidance or financial support, which is especially relevant for those men who have migrated away from the home for employment. Regardless of their contribution, when men are actively involved in family life and do not differentiate between "women's work" and "men's work," everyone in the household benefits.

Key Resources

Connell, R. (2014) Margin becoming centre: For a world-centred rethinking of masculinities, *NORMA: International Journal for Masculinity Studies*, 9(4): 217-231.

Hussey, M. (ed) (2003) *Masculinities: Interdisciplinary readings.* Upper Saddle River, NJ: Prentice Hall.

Jackson, R.L. and Balaji, M. (eds) (2013) *Global masculinities and manhood.* Champaign, IL: University of Illinois Press.

Kaufman, M.A. (2002) *Taking the field: Women, men, and sports.* Minneapolis, MN: University of Minnesota Press.

Kimmel, M.S., Hearn, J. and Connell, R. (eds) (2005) *Handbook of studies on men and masculinities.* Thousand Oaks, CA: Sage.

Koc, Y. and Vignoles, V.L. (2016) Global identification predicts gay-male identity and well-being among Turkish gay men, *British Journal of Social Psychology*, 55(4): 643-661.

Ramamurthy, P. (2010) Why Are Men Doing Floral Sex Work? Gender, Cultural Reproduction, and the Feminization of Agriculture, *Signs*, 35(2): 397-424.

Ruspini, E., Hearn, J., Pease, B. and Pringle, K. (eds) (2011) *Men and masculinities around the world: Transforming men's practices*, New York, NY: Palgrave Macmillan.

Sarti, R. and Scrinzi, F. (2010) Introduction to the Special Issue: Men in a Woman's Job, Male Domestic Workers, International Migration and the Globalization of Care, *Men and Masculinities*, 13(1): 4-15.

Trujillo, N. (1991) Hegemonic Masculinity on the Mound: Media Representations of Nolan Ryan and American Sports Culture, *Critical Studies in Mass Communication*, 8(3): 290–308.

Whitehead, S., Barrett, F.J. and Kociatkiewicz, J. (eds) (2001) *The Masculinities reader*, Maldon, MA: Polity.

World Health Organization (2017) World health statistics 2017: Monitoring health for the SDGs, Sustainable Development Goals, Retrieved March 5, 2018 (http://www.who.int/gho/publications/world_health_statistics/2017/en/).

NINE

Lack of Access to Comprehensive Sexuality Education

Jacqueline Daugherty and Richelle Frabotta,
Miami University

The Problem

The lack of access to Comprehensive Sexuality Education (CSE) is a serious social problem for the majority of the world's population. It is well known that rates of other social problems, such as unintended pregnancies, sexually transmitted infections, and vulnerability to coercive relationships, decline when people have access to CSE. Though it is difficult to measure how many students receive formal or school-based CSE, there is data aplenty of the dangerous knowledge deficits that happen without CSE access. For example, UNESCO estimates that only 34 % of young people around the world can demonstrate accurate knowledge of HIV prevention and transmission.

It is only within the last two decades that the case for CSE as a human right, and not simply an instrument of risk reduction, has been popularized. International treaties (e.g., UN Convention to End All Forms of Discrimination Against Women) recognize that all people have a right to accurate information about sex and sexuality because they have the right to make the best decisions for them.

UNESCO defines Comprehensive Sexuality Education (CSE) as *an age-appropriate, culturally relevant approach to teaching about sexuality and relationships by providing scientifically accurate, realistic, non-judgmental information.* The United Nations (UN) and the World Health Organization (WHO) have invested in research that supports the school and community-based implementation of CSE in all global regions. Despite this global commitment and the vast body of scientific research that supports it, CSE remains under-mandated, under-implemented, and overly controversial in most places. A few quick points provide a global snapshot of CSE access:

- Global: There is very little data on the quality of or number of 10–14-year-old students receiving CSE, despite the fact that most of those students live in countries with CSE policy commitments.
- USA: Since 2006, adolescent access to CSE has been on the decline. This decline is unsurprising, given that the share of schools providing sexual health education declined between 2000 and 2014.
- European Union: European Union member states have differences in quality and frequency of CSE, with The Netherlands and Scandinavian countries hosting the highest quality programming and Eastern Europe consistently missing the mark.

Where are the challenges in mandating and implementing CSE with consistency of quality and curriculum? The following three sub-sections under Research Evidence outline key barriers to CSE access around the globe and demonstrate the scope of the problem. The chapter ends with solutions to these barriers that have been evaluated in practice, and some core recommendations on where we should go from here.

Research Evidence

CSE National Policy Mandates Are Non-existent or Suffer Serious Implementation Challenges

A nation's policy ideally reflects its priorities. As global support for CSE grows, there are still major challenges in education sector CSE policy adoption and implementation that includes variation among and within nations. Some nations have no mandate for CSE (e.g., United States). Others have a mandate or other formal commitment, but have issues in effectively operationalizing that policy (e.g., Guatemala, Kenya). Still others—a minority of nations to be sure—have long had national CSE mandates and enjoy the success of an effective, compulsory, and continuous program (e.g., Sweden).

The US is unique among wealthy Global North countries in that the federal government has no national policy mandating sexuality education, and support for certain types of sex education change as frequently as presidential administrations. The George W. Bush administration (2000–2008) heavily favored Abstinence-Only-Until-

Marriage sex education (AOUM, see the next section for details), whereas the Obama administration (2008–2016) put far more support toward CSE, and all indications are that the Trump administration (2016 onwards) is swinging back to AOUM. As a result, state education policies vary widely, and can also be subject to political whim rather than an evidence-driven approach. Below is a brief snapshot of state sex education policy variation in the US, via the Guttmacher Institute's comprehensive and updated repository of state policies.

- Less than half of all states (24) require sex education in schools
- 36 states allow parents to remove children from instruction
- 26 states require that information on abstinence be stressed
- 18 states require provision of contraception information
- Of the 12 states that require discussion of sexual orientation, 3 specify that schools disseminate only negative information about it and only 4 mandate gender identity coverage.

Given these numbers, the general decline in US student exposure to CSE in recent years is unsurprising.

The 2015 UNESCO global review of CSE analyzes previous research on CSE in 48 countries, most of which are developing and in the Global South. It found that although nearly 80% of these countries have policies or strategies that support CSE, there remains a significant gap between the policies in place and the actual implementation on the ground. For example, Guatemala has a legal and policy framework that supports CSE in primary and secondary schools as part of the 2008 Latin American and Caribbean ministerial declaration, *Preventing through Education*. Yet, teacher training and school programming suffers a severe lack of support due to "insufficient political will and budgets."

Budget priorities are not just a problem in Guatemala, as budget policy and austerity play an increasing role in inability to access CSE in wealthy Global North countries. In the US context, Planned Parenthood—a major CSE provider—was barred from receiving any federal funding in President Trump's proposed 2018 budget because the organization also provides abortion services. Some states such as Ohio have attempted to ban Planned Parenthood from eligibility for state funds as well, though those efforts have largely been overturned by federal courts. A 2013 European Union Report on its sex education policies recognized that the wide variation of quality and frequency of delivery of sex education across member states can partially be attributed to austerity-driven public-sector budget cuts. The report clarifies that those states with sex education deficiencies have also been disproportionately impacted by these cuts.

CSE Often Challenges Traditionalist Cultural Expectations

Another primary challenge to CSE access around the globe is the strength of the following cultural norms: the prioritization of morality over scientific research on matters of education and sexual and reproductive health and traditionalist discourses on gender and sexual identity, power, and pleasure in regards to sexual decision making and resource access. The stronger and more integrated into social institutions these norms are, the less access young people will have access to CSE. This is because CSE's provision of non-judgmental and scientifically accurate information threatens many religious and cultural beliefs, for example, about sex's primary purpose as reproduction, marriage as the only or best context for sexual activity, and the problematic treatment of diverse sexual identities. Leading CSE advocacy organizations, such as the United Nations and Guttmacher Institute, agree that these cultural norms often help to decrease CSE access.

First, a school's prioritization of religious or other morality-based perspectives on sexuality over those derived from scientific research is most often a barrier to CSE. At worst, morality-based perspectives serve as central arguments for why sex education shouldn't be taught at all in schools. At best, the disregard for scientifically based information cultivates a sex education that is fraught with dangerous misinformation and that puts students at risk even as it purports to help them. This second point is perhaps best illustrated by the continued prevalence of Abstinence-Only-Until-Marriage (AOUM) education in the United States. AOUM is touted as an alternative to CSE and is defined by the Sexuality Information and Education Council of the United States as sexuality education that prioritizes the promotion of heterosexual marriage as the only appropriate context for sexual activity and rarely includes accurate information on condoms, birth control/condom use, consent, and healthy relationships. It grew out of a US cultural backlash against CSE in schools and is largely designed from a conservative Christian perspective that advocates for sexual "chastity" and "purity" until marriage, as evidenced by the title of a popular AOUM curriculum *True Love Waits*. The US federal government has spent over $2 billion on domestic AOUM programming and required that $1.4 billion of PEPFAR programming aid be spent on AOUM to prevent HIV transmission in sub-Saharan Africa. And comprehensive studies of AOUM's impact domestically and abroad have consistently shown its failure to delay onset of first intercourse experience, prevent HIV, or increase the likelihood to abstain from sex. Yet both US state and federal support for domestic AOUM programs continues—stronger in some regions than others—and only 13 of 50 states require that any sex education is medically accurate. This may lead one to believe that CSE delivery in schools is the solution to this problem, and though CSE is the core part of the solution, cultural challenges in its delivery still exist. In Eastern and Southern Africa, teachers trained in CSE still report discomfort in addressing issues of condoms and masturbation in the classroom as frank and open discussion of these topics are against cultural norms in many places.

Second, and related to this priority on morality over science, is the power of traditionalist discourses on gender and sexual identity and pleasure in regards to sexual decision making and resource access. These discourses include, but are not limited to, women's primary role as mothers and wives, sexual pleasure (especially for women) as wrong or unimportant, and the denial of recognition to people of diverse gender and sexual identities. The United States yields notable examples of the ways in which these discourses block access to effective CSE. A 2004 federal government sponsored study of the most commonly funded AOUM curricula, known as the Waxman Report, found that many curricula treat gender stereotypes as scientific fact. One curricula, for example, teaches that "Women gauge their happiness and judge their success on their relationships. Men's happiness and success hinge on their accomplishments." However, some CSE curricula also reproduce social inequalities. For example, the rights and experiences of LGBTQ youth and the discussion on sexual pleasure is often subordinated to the primary goals of unplanned pregnancy prevention and infection risk reduction. Many countries in Eastern Europe and Central Asia rarely acknowledge the specific sexual and reproductive health needs/ rights of young people with disabilities and LGBTQ youth in CSE programming. Similarly, despite its national CSE policy commitment, Kenyan teachers report delivery challenges that range from inadequate teacher training to widely held personal beliefs that conflict with CSE standards. For example, 96% of Kenyan teachers in one survey believed that relationships should only be between a man and a woman and only a slightly lower proportion believed that young people should abstain from sex until marriage. Unsurprisingly, only 1 in 4 Kenyan teens report learning about contraception.

Researchers, educators, and CSE advocates around the world have recognized that effective CSE must be evidence-based and both inclusive and non-stigmatizing. It should address sexual violence, and make central gender and sexual identity equity. Fields summarizes the solution when she insists that all sex education should promote social and sexual justice.

CSE Classroom Delivery is Inconsistent and Not Student-Centered

A majority of countries now embrace the concept of CSE, informed by evidence and international guidance, and are working to strengthen its implementation at a national level. Two major components of CSE implementation and delivery are effective teaching preparation and age-appropriate, developmentally relevant curricula standards. Since cultural variations exist in drastic difference among global nations, alignment on these two components is difficult at best and appropriate attention should be given to both.

Ensuring standardized and sexuality-specific training for teachers is essential for curricula delivery and student success. It should be no secret that well-prepared teachers are key to effective sexuality instruction. In countries like the US where there is no CSE policy mandate, curriculum standardization is nearly impossible and therefore pre-service or in-service teacher training is rare. However, teacher training is also a major challenge for countries that have national policy mandates and/or CSE guidelines available. For example, Peru has had national CSE guidelines in place since 2008 and strong school administration and parent support for CSE, yet CSE delivery is far behind the country's stated goals. Only about 9% of students learned about topics in all five areas of Peru's CSE Guidelines, and there are wide gaps among students in critical areas such as contraception and sexual violence. In fact one multi-regional study found that 25% of Peruvian students thought that when young women say no to sex, they really mean yes. These knowledge gaps are unsurprising when one learns that less than half of teachers surveyed had access to lesson plans and textbooks on the subject. Less than half received pre-service training on sexuality education. Similarly, research from ten countries in Eastern and Southern Africa found that most teacher training curricula did not mention access to guidance, supervision or reporting requirements for teachers who encountered disclosure of sexual abuse during delivery of sexuality education programs, pointing to a critical lack of supervision and support.

Recommendations and Solutions

Compulsory, well-funded and successfully operationalized school and community-based CSE programming is the primary answer to the problems caused by non-mandated, voluntary, and inconsistent or nonexistent sexuality education. These efforts must be grounded in *evidence-based curriculum standardization and assessment and subsequent teacher training on those standards are key to removing both cultural and delivery barriers.*

The Netherlands and Sweden serve as shining examples. They have mandated school-based CSE for decades and enjoy some of the lowest unplanned pregnancy and STI rates and highest gender equity outcome scores in the world. The Dutch sexuality education curriculum starts at age 4 and stretches into late adolescence. It focuses both on technical information such as sexual and reproductive anatomy and physiology and a rights-based approach in which diverse gender and sexual identities are represented. There are national guidelines, but regional differences exist because educational sectors in different parts of the country have the opportunity to localize the information presented, but within the scope of the national guidelines. Teacher training is built into post-secondary teacher education. A 2011 UNESCO Report praised its holistic approach because it considers "all stages of sexual, social, emotional and physical development of children." Sweden's program is similar in purpose and structure, but also allows for NGO involvement in school-based programming and has utilized community-based youth programs that reinforce messaging in schools. Both countries are held up as CSE models and have served as an example of how well CSE can work when the necessary commitment and resources are put forth.

As we have learned, challenges remain for the rest of the world. From the lack of political will and fund commitment to teacher training deficits to continued lags in global secondary school enrollment, non-govermental organizations and creative university partnerships are vital in leading and supplementing government efforts to remove obstacles to CSE access.

- Feminist and other rights-based NGOs continue to center CSE access at all levels of international policy and implementation. One example is the development of the 2009 *International Technical Guidance on Sexuality Education*, which serves as the foundation for most regional ministerial and other CSE policy commitments.
- Digital initiatives, such as the recently launched Real Talk mobile phone app for middle schoolers created by two US doctoral students,

that provide CSE designed by health professionals and informed by teens, circumvent the traditional policy/implementation problems.

- The Future of Sex Education (FoSE)—an NGO collaborative—is working with some US educators and districts to implement the national sexuality education standards they developed in the absence of government leadership on the issue.

- *Abriendo Oportunidades* (Opening Opportunities) is an NGO in Guatemala whose mentorship program has seen success in educating teen girls—often not in school—on their options concerning reproductive health and sexual violence. University–community partnership initiatives, such as the Sexuality Education Studies Center at Miami University, are linking academic research and content experts with front-line CSE providers and policy makers in order to train and mentor future teachers and other human service professionals in CSE. The American Association of Sexuality Educators, Counselors and Therapists (AASECT) is an international NGO that requires a Sexual Attitude Reassessment (SAR) as part of its Certified Sexuality Educator credentialing process. The SAR is a structured, multi-day workshop that explores one's personal sex, sexuality concerns, fears, and trauma. The training is key to delivering medically-accurate and culturally competent material with the student's learning and developing worldview fore fronted. This teacher training is key for effective CSE implementation.

CSE access is key to both sexual risk reduction and the recognition that every person has the right to decide what is best for their own bodies across the lifespan.

Key References

Beaumont, K. and Maguire, M. (2013) *European Parliament Report: Policies for Sex Education in the European Union.* European Union: Brussels. Retrieved from: http://www.europarl.europa.eu/studies

Fields, J. (2008) *Risky Lessons: Sex Education and Social Inequality*, New Brunswick, N.J.: Rutgers University Press.

Future of Sex Education Initiative (2012) National Sexuality Education Standards: Core Content and Skills, K-12, A special publication of the *Journal of School Health.* Retrieved from http://www. futureofsexeducation. org/documents/josh-fose-standards-web.pdf

Guttmacher Institute (no date) International Teens: Comprehensive Sexuality Education, Retrieved from: https://www.guttmacher.org/international/teens/comprehensive-sexuality-education

Guttmacher Institute (2018) State Laws and Policies: Sex and HIV Education, Retrieved from: https://www.guttmacher.org/state-policy/explore/sex-and-hiv-education

HHS and Centers for Disease Control and Prevention (2015) *Results from the School Health Policies and Practices Study 2014*, https://www.cdc.gov/healthyyouth/data/shpps/pdf/shpps-508-final_101315.pdf

Lindberg, L., Boonstra, H. and Maddow-Zimet, I. (2016) Change in Adolescent Receipt of Sex Education, 2006-2013, *Journal of Adolescent Health*, 58(6): 621-627.

Santelli, J.S, Kantor, L.M., Grilo, S.A., Speizer, I.S., Lindberg, L.D. et al (2017) Abstinence-Only-Until-Marriage: An Updated Review of U.S. Policies and Programs and Their Impact, *Journal of Adolescent Health,* 61: 273-280.

Sitron, J.A. and Dyson, D. (2009) Sexuality Attitudes Reassessment (SAR): Historical and New Considerations for Measuring its Effectiveness American, *Journal of Sexuality Education*, 4: 158–177.

UNESCO (2009) *International Technical Guidance on Sexuality Education: An Evidence-informed Approach for Schools, Teachers and Health Educators*, vols 1 and 2. UNESCO: Paris. Retrieved from: http://portal.unesco.org/en/ev.php-URL_ID=47268&URL_DO=DO_TOPIC&URL_SECTION=201.html

UNESCO (2015) *Emerging Evidence, Lessons and Practice in Comprehensive Sexuality Education: A Global Review*. UNESCO: Paris, France. Retrieved from http://unesdoc.unesco.org/images/0024/002431/243106e.pdf

Key Resources

American Association of Sexuality Educators, Counselors and Therapists: http://www.aasect.org

Sexuality Information and Education Council of the United States: http://www.siecus.org

Advocates for Youth: http://www.advocatesforyouth.org

SECTION IV

Violence Against Precarious Groups

TEN

Violence Against Migrants: A Global Analysis[1]

Rosemary Barberet and Diana Rodriguez-Spahia,
John Jay College of Criminal Justice

The Problem

Violence against migrants is an escalating social problem globally. According to the International Organization for Migration, a migrant is anyone that is "moving or has moved across an international border, whether the movement is voluntary or involuntary." The World Migration Report 2018 notes that "in recent years, we have seen an increase in migration and displacement occurring due to conflict, persecution, environmental degradation and change, and a profound lack of human security and opportunity." The problem outlined in this chapter is that migrants, depending on their level of vulnerability to victimization, experience different types of violence during multiple phases of migration, and existing policies are often insufficient to reduce the violence. We will offer examples of the unique types of violence that migrants may experience from each continent.

There are distinct factors that cause someone to leave their country of origin. Push factors are those that force individuals to leave in hopes of an improved life elsewhere, such as overpopulation, poverty, crime, and armed conflict. Pull factors are elements that attract migration to a destination country, such as work-related opportunities. Both push and pull factors create opportunities for violence against migrants. People may also be trafficked, and often leave their countries because they are deceived by traffickers which creates a unique host of issues.

[1] Support for this project was provided by PSC-CUNY Award 64276-00 42, jointly funded by The Professional Staff Congress and The City University of New York.

Violence perpetrated against migrants globally occurs before, during, and after migration. Violence against migrants can also happen anywhere: in transit, in the workplace, at home, in refugee camps or detention centers, and within migrant groups. Many States deny rights to migrants. Irregular status is common and has severe repercussions such as deportation and statelessness. Denial of rights and irregular status often lead to economic and social marginalization. In the workplace, abuse and violence are common and may include: underpay, withholding of pay, hazardous work conditions, and sexual and physical abuse. Within and outside of the workplace, migrants are subject to violence from verbal abuse to murder. One reason is xenophobia: the perpetrators of violence are antagonistic towards non-natives. Workplace managers and others take advantage of the precarious position in which migrants find themselves: they are frequently poor, desperate for income, and do not often report crimes or abuse to law enforcement.

Violence against migrants is not always perpetrated by a non-migrant. Migrants also suffer violence within their groups. Intimate partner violence (IPV) is one of the most common types of violence perpetrated among migrants. Although IPV can be perpetrated against men, women are the principal victims of these crimes, which go largely unreported. IPV among migrants is understood in the literature as a phenomenon that stems from culturally embedded patriarchal beliefs and may also be the result of adaptation stressors: low income and low education. Violence against children may also take place, and children may be abused in the home and at school.

Research Evidence

Africa

- The ongoing instability and conflicts in many countries on the African continent are a partial cause of xenophobic behaviors.
- There is a high level of xenophobia: as an example, Somali migrants are especially targeted in South Africa.
- Native populations accuse migrants of stealing their work opportunities, and this leads to street violence, violent demonstrations against migrant workers, and even gender-based violence in the form of rape of female migrant workers.
- Newcomers are excluded from communities, and this adds to the isolation and the challenges faced.

Asia

- Migrants are subject to types of violence such as home confinement or denial of right to travel; political leaders have been known to lead demonstrations and incite violence against migrants.
- Asia has a high rate of suicide among migrants.
- Violence against women and children in migrant families is high.
- Migrant women in Hong Kong are reported to be extremely vulnerable to IPV, and a society tolerant to these behaviors compounds the prevalence of this problem.

Australia

- Australia's immigration rate has been cited as among the highest in the world.
- Migrants have reported racially motivated victimization.
- Violence in the workplace occurs in orchards via backbreaking work: long work shifts in extreme conditions without breaks, reduced pay, and physical abuse.
- In addition to workplace violence, there are high rates of domestic violence among migrants.

Europe

- Migrants in Europe face problems such as domestic and structural violence which is perpetrated by a social institution and prevents these groups from being able to obtain basic needs and causes harm (i.e. border-based or legislative in nature), and xenophobic/hate-motivated violence which is often perpetrated by far-right groups.
- There is also high incidence of victimization of children of migrants, or children that are first generation migrants themselves through bullying, exclusion, and physical violence.

Latin America and the Caribbean

- There is a high rate of street violence against migrants.
- Drug gangs have been known to kidnap and murder migrants.
- Activists advocating for the rights of migrants are also targets of violent crime.

- Migrants in these areas report constant fear of and victimization by gang robbery, harassment, and extortion by law enforcement and border authorities.
- In addition to the concerns they face outside of the home, migrants in Latin America and the Caribbean also face domestic violence at home.
- Structural violence has also been reported between the United States and Mexico, namely in the form of violence perpetrated by border officers and police.

Middle East

- Domestic servants tend to be women and are routinely denied their rights such as being locked inside their workplaces and have their travel documents confiscated by employers.
- Migrant workers, mostly men, work in construction and labor and are beaten by supervisors.
- The International Labor Organization has reported that over 600,000 people live in conditions of forced labor in this region.
- Syrian refugees are the target of violence in many countries around the world, such as in Lebanon, where there is increasing intolerance toward them.
- Women are routinely the victims of sexual violence and exploitation in Jordanian refugee camps, and young girls are subject to child marriage in Jordanian refugee camps to alleviate families of dishonor associated with rape.

North America

- Migrants face harassment and profiling from law enforcement and border authorities. At the United States–Mexico border, violent bands of vigilantes assault and harass migrants.
- Gender-based violence is also reported by female migrant workers, who are exploited because of their irregular status and fear of reporting crime.
- "Border towns" (along the U.S.–Mexico border) are also known to have very high rates of domestic violence.
- Children of migrant workers are also affected and there is a great deal of research about violence experienced in and out of the home.

Children and adolescents also experience bullying and violence at school.

Recommendations and Solutions

Migrants, particularly illegalized migrants, are a vulnerable population regardless of their country of origin or destination. Not only do they experience discrimination and abuse at their origin country and from natives of the destination country, they also experience violence en route, in refugee camps and detention centers, and in the home among themselves. Migrant groups often have few resources, little financial support, and cannot count on law enforcement or the criminal justice system to provide assistance. As these problems have slowly come to light, several solutions have been suggested by the literature to reduce instances of all kinds of violence against migrants. Below is a summary of the most effective solutions to prevent this violence.

1. *Provide resources of all kinds to migrant communities.*
Migrants are especially in need of outreach programs that can assist in: networking with other migrants that have successfully integrated into the destination country, language-learning programs, legal advice, and mental health counseling. Assistance with finding jobs is also critical to their successful settlement and integration. Introducing them to migrants that have settled successfully may allow newcomers to feel that they have a network they can look to for camaraderie, assistance, and advisement. Learning the native language of the destination country is deeply important as it can help migrants in better communication, and better jobs. Legal advice is an indispensable need as migrants can be empowered and encouraged to take legal action against those that have victimized them. Lastly, mental health counseling that is culturally sensitive is one of the options that can help prevent violence among migrants by providing assistance with problems in adapting to their new environments and with triggers and cultural mindsets that lead to domestic violence.

2. *Involve community leaders.*
In order to ensure that outreach programs outlined above are effective, it is critical to involve community leaders such as health and human services personnel, legal and law enforcement administrators, and religious and grassroots organizations and agencies. The persons listed above are in the best position to assist migrants due to the fact

that migrants are most likely to need assistance in these fields, and individually, these practitioners can ensure that migrants know these resources are available to them. Also, culture may dictate which types of assistance migrants may seek, so including religious and grassroots organizations, and not just "official" groups such as law enforcement and human services is key. Many migrants, especially those fleeing from human rights violations, civil conflict, or those that are in dire socio-economic conditions need to be able to receive direction and counsel from persons they trust most and feel most comfortable with.

3.   *Create publicity campaigns at the community level to ensure that migrants are aware of resources that are available.*

A common theme in the literature is that migrants were unaware that resources were available to them. Publicity campaigns may include announcements on television, free magazines, or strategically placed ads in workplaces that are likely to have migrants—doctor's offices, communities with high populations of migrants, or places where migrants may congregate socially such as bars, parks, or cafes. Another publicity campaign is to create public information events held several times a year in easily accessible public locations such as town squares which would consist of several booths or kiosks with representatives of community leaders ready to speak with attendants of the events, or to provide them with informational pamphlets and resources such as forms, telephone numbers, or websites. When available, smart phones can also be an indispensable tool for migrants to obtain information about border safety, locations of camps and services, and to obtain timely news about any dangers throughout their journey and at their destination. Social media can also be an excellent way to obtain information, and for migrants to maintain communication with the families they may have left behind.

4.   *Develop culturally specific intervention programs with peer educators.*

The vulnerability of these groups may make them distrustful of "outsiders", and so peer educators located in communities that are heavily populated with migrants may be a solution to simultaneously build a network of support and trust, and also educate and provide key resources. The literature also suggests that these programs and interventions should be culturally specific. As previously indicated, a pervasive form of violence against migrants is actually in the form of domestic violence within their groups caused by culturally embedded patriarchy. Therefore, for intervention and education programs to be successful, they must be culturally sensitive and specific. Some migrants may feel more at ease pursuing channels that are even more informal in nature, so having peer educators to help them navigate this difficult process in a way that is deemed culturally acceptable is key and may act as the stepping stone to trust community leaders.

5. Create programs geared toward migrant schoolchildren.

Migrant children also witness violence or experience it directly, yet they are a group of migrants that are often neglected in research and practice. Therefore, there should be programs and interventions at schools that not only aid children that may be experiencing violence in the home via mental health counseling that is culturally sensitive, but school staff and security must be trained to handle bullying and other types of violence in the school setting for which migrant children may be particularly at risk. Schools should also formulate clear and actionable plans to report abuse children experience in the home, and to handle bullying of migrant children within their walls.

6. Remove institutional barriers.

Often, institutional barriers are the culprit of what must be removed in order for migrants to feel more comfortable seeking assistance. Specifically, legislators should review and modify laws in the areas of education, migration, housing, transport, and criminal justice as this will provide the most benefit. Laws may be outdated and may not address the new types of problems migrants face, nor their breadth. Further, their enforcement mechanisms may lack the training, incentive or resources necessary to ensure they are in fact closely acted upon.

7. Update/implement training of key personnel.

First responders such as police officers need training to effectively and ethically respond to the unique issues migrants may be facing, and sensitivity training should be implemented as well. A significant amount of violence faced by migrants is structural in nature. Structural violence includes treatment at borders, in detention centers, the law enforcement response to migration, or even laws in place that are discriminatory or harmful to migrants. Therefore, it is the personnel typically responsible that are in the greatest need of (re)training; the consequences should they deviate from ethical and legal behavior should be clearly communicated and enforced. Globally, impunity of perpetrators of violence against migrants, migrant workers, and their families is high. Further, it is often difficult to uncover who is committing these crimes because they are severely underreported.

When coupled with the fear felt by victims for reporting these crimes, this results in difficulty establishing the characteristics of offenders.

8. *Implement special services for human trafficking victims.*

Some migrants may have left their country of origin under conditions of human trafficking, which makes them particularly vulnerable. Their travel documents are often seized, they are threatened, beaten, and coerced. These victims are also forced to work and are often exploited in the sex, labor, and construction industries. Labor laws should require employers to be vigilant and protective of potential trafficking victims. Awareness campaigns in both countries of origin and destination are essential to prevent trafficking and to recognize and assist victims. Training of those in the transportation industry and law enforcement, customs, and borders is also key to identify victims. Services for victims must be adapted to the special needs of trafficking victims.

9. *Recognize human rights of migrants.*

The Office of the United Nations High Commissioner for Human Rights (OHCHR) has recognized that migrants are routinely stripped of their human rights via the countless acts of discrimination and exploitation we have outlined in this chapter. They often experience denial of freedom, education, and healthcare due to discriminatory attitudes and laws. They may also be denied their human rights before they arrive to their destinations. As an example, law enforcement and border patrol may be instructed to arrest illegal migrants and send them to detention centers which are often in deplorable conditions before they are ultimately deported. Law enforcement practices/ customs need to be reevaluated to ensure they are meeting global human rights standards.

10. *Support global cooperation.*

In September 2016, the United Nations General Assembly hosted a high-level Summit for Refugees and Migrants. At this Summit, all 193 Member States of the United Nations unanimously adopted the New York Declaration for Refugees and Migrants (Resolution 71/1). The New York Declaration lays the groundwork for further action to improve the situation of refugees and migrants by laying out a process for the development of two "global compacts," one on refugees and the other for safe, orderly, and regular migration, which are to be adopted in 2018. This declaration and these global compacts are a significant global step forward in addressing the problems experienced by migrants in our research report. Internationally, countries need to follow suit and take seriously the international standards signed and agreed upon to protect and uplift these particularly vulnerable groups present in virtually every country. This is not "someone else's" problem: it is everyone's problem.

Sources For Further Reading:

Antonopoulos, G.A. (2006) Greece: Policing Racist Violence in The 'Fenceless Vineyard', *Race & Class*, 48(2): 92–100.

Bjereld, Y., Daneback, K. and Petzold, M. (2014) Differences in Prevalence of Bullying Victimization Between Native and Immigrant Children in the Nordic Countries: A Parent-Reported Serial Cross-Sectional Study, *Child: Care, Health and Development*, 41(4): 593–599.

Cepeda, A., Negi, N., Nowotny, K., Arango, J., Kaplan, C. and Valdez, A. (2012) Social Stressors, Special Vulnerabilities, and Violence Victimization among Latino Immigrant Day Laborers in Post-Katrina New Orleans, in M. Zatz, C.E. Kubrin and R. Martinez, (eds) *Punishing Immigrants: Policy, Politics, and Injustice*, New York University Press, pp 207–231.

Erez, E., Adelman, M. and Gregory, C. (2009) Intersections of Immigration and Domestic Violence: Voices of Battered Immigrant Women, *Feminist Criminology*, 4(1): 32–56.

Gonçalves, M. and Matos, M. (2016) Prevalence of Violence against Immigrant Women: A Systematic Review of the Literature, *Journal of Family Violence*, 31(6): 697–710.

Infante, C., Idrovo, A.J., Sánchez-Domínguez, M.S., Vinhas, S. and González Vázquez, T. (2012) Violence Committed Against Migrants in Transit: Experiences on the Northern Mexican Border, *Journal of Immigrant and Minority Health*, 14(3): 449–459.

Nagai, M., Karunakara, U., Rowley, E. and Burnham, G. (2008) Violence Against Refugees, Non-Refugees and Host Populations in Southern Sudan and Northern Uganda, *Global Public Health*, 3(3): 249–270.

Silva, A. and Massey, D. (2015) Violence, Networks, and International Migration from Colombia, *International Organization For Migration*, 53(5): 1–17.

Turner-Moss, E., Zimmerman, C., Howard, L.M., and Oram, S. (2013) Labour Exploitation and Health: A Case Series of Men and Women Seeking Post-Trafficking Services, *Journal of Immigrant and Minority Health*, 16(3): 473–480.

Walsh, S.D., De Clercq, B., Molcho, M., Harel-Fisch, Y., Davison, C.M., Rich Madsen, K. and Stevens, G. (2016) The Relationship Between Immigrant School Composition, Classmate Support and Involvement in Physical Fighting and Bullying Among Adolescent Immigrants and Non-immigrants in 11 Countries, *Journal of Youth and Adolescence*, 45(1): 1–16.

ELEVEN

Sex Workers and Coping with Violence: Implications for Policy-Making

Mangala Subramaniam, Zachary D. Palmer,
and Vasundhara Kaul, Purdue University, West Lafayette

The Problem

Around the world, women involved in sex work (henceforth sex workers), irrespective of whether they are street-based, brothel-based, or home-based, disproportionately experience gender-based violence. The forms of violence faced by sex workers vary across types of sex work (for instance, home-based versus street-based) and range from physical, emotional, and sexual abuse by clients, non-paying intimate partners, and by police. According to the World Health Organization (WHO), many sex workers consider violence "normal" or "part of the job" and therefore are often reluctant to report incidences of rapes, murder (attempted or otherwise), beatings, molestation, or sexual assault to authorities.

Violence is a manifestation of the stigma and discrimination experienced by sex workers; it transcends international borders. Laws governing prostitution and law enforcement authorities are key to mitigating the violence experienced by sex workers. In most countries, sex work is either illegal or has an ambiguous legal status. For example, in India and the United Kingdom, prostitution is not illegal, but procurement of sex workers and soliciting in public is illegal. That is, in India, it is legal to offer sexual services to anyone for money. However, this must be a direct trade. A third party cannot take commission from the woman's earnings by maintaining brothels or pimping. Sex workers are therefore, frequently regarded as easy targets for harassment and violence by clients, partners, the public, and the police as they are considered immoral and deserving of punishment. The WHO also notes that sex work is associated with a high risk of HIV infection because the prevalence of violence and HIV/AIDS are

103

interlinked. In this chapter, we discuss the problem of violence against sex workers and make eight recommendations for solutions to help combat this global issue.

Research Evidence

Research from Bangladesh, Namibia, India, and elsewhere, as reported by WHO, shows that many sex workers, particularly those who work on the streets, report being beaten, threatened with a weapon, slashed, choked, raped, and coerced into sex. However, perpetrators of the violence vary. A report of FHI 360, a nonprofit human development organization, notes that a large percentage of sex workers from across the world report various acts of aggression by a variety of perpetrators: physical or sexual abuse by clients (8–76%); physical or sexual violence from non-paying intimate partners (4–64%); sexual violence by police (7–89%); and physical violence by police (5–100%). In Bangladesh, 94% of sex workers have experienced violence from a range of perpetrators including clients, gatekeepers, police, main partners, and neighbors, according to a WHO report.

Many sex workers consider violence to be normal or part of the job and do not have information about their rights. As a result, they are often reluctant to report incidences of rapes, attempted (or actual) murders, beatings, molestation, or sexual assault to the authorities. Even when they do report, their claims are often dismissed. For example, WHO notes that studies among street-based sex workers in Vancouver, Canada, and in New York City show that a majority of incidences of harassment, assault, rape, kidnapping, and murder are not reported to the police. Where they are reported, the police do not register the complaints and in the few instances where they are registered, the perpetrators are not convicted. Moreover, research from Indonesia and India shows that sex workers who are rounded up during police raids are beaten, coerced into having sex by corrupt police officials in exchange for their release or placed in institutions where they are sexually exploited or physically abused. The raids also drive sex workers onto the streets where they are more vulnerable to violence.

Extramarital sexual partnerships are a common reason for violence among sex workers. Both cohabiting partners and non-cohabiting partners may be perpetrators of violence against sex workers. As posited by gender scholars, violence is about a struggle for power as well as control over earnings, pressure to earn more, and a sense of superiority. These issues also emerge in the research of the first author about the violence faced by sex workers in Southern India. Many sex workers who do not disclose their identity rely on partners—cohabiting or not—for emotional support but this arrangement has often led to struggles over control of money and power.

The problem of violence against sex workers is also linked to larger public health issues. The WHO notes that sex work is associated with an increased risk of HIV infection, in part because the prevalence of violence and HIV/AIDS are interlinked. Gender inequality is one major risk factor identified in studies of violence faced by sex workers and which in turn also raises their risks to HIV. The growing recognition of the relationship between gender inequality and violence and the related risk to HIV has resulted in a concomitant rise in more gender-specific interventions across countries. In many countries, women's entry into sex work is attributed not only to poverty but gender inequality and violence perpetrated particularly by men. Hence, some interventions specifically target young men to reduce violence against women by challenging norms of masculinity (examples are, One Man Can and Program H). Others seek to empower women by building knowledge of sexual health, communication skills, and through microfinance initiatives (examples are, IMAGE and SHAZ!). Uniquely, Stepping Stones works with both men and women, dividing them into peer groups and then bringing them together to build stronger, more gender-equitable relationships with better communication between partners.

There are additional examples of gender transformative programs. They include the One Man Can (OMC) Campaign which was designed and implemented by Sonke Gender Justice Network, an NGO in South Africa, aimed to examine the links between gender, power, and health. In a similar vein, the focus of Program H, developed by Instituto Promundo in Brazil, uses a group educational format with young men to challenge male norms of violence and multiple partners within a safe environment facilitated by a male role model.

The attention to gender in these programs is laudable as it circumscribes the lives of some women's entry into sex work and their experiences of violence. But they adopt an individual level approach to address gender rather than focus on the structurally embedded forms of gender relations within the family and society. By not accounting for structural factors, that is societal and institutional norms (such as within families) of gender as well as poverty that push some women into sex work and expose them to violence, interventions overlook a major aspect of risk faced by women.

Recommendations and Solutions

1. *We call for grassroots campaign efforts to transform cultural understandings of sex work and the violence associated with it.* International agencies, national governments, and non-governmental organizations (NGOs) can develop campaigns to educate policy makers, the public, and police personnel about sex work and sex workers. Some grassroots campaign efforts can include street plays particularly in public spaces in urban and semi-urban areas to educate the public. In addition, programs for youth may be meaningful as younger generations are more likely to be receptive to such information. The campaigns should focus on the different types of sex work (such as street-based versus brothel-based) and the varying conditions in which they work such as the major role of pimps in brothel-based sex work. In addition, campaigns should also be geared towards advocating for change in the ways that violence against sex workers is typically viewed (i.e., that violence is normal).

2. *We call for targeting change in structures of social inequality by mobilized and organized groups of sex workers.* Addressing violence faced by sex workers must consider the structural basis of power and address gender inequality. Structurally embedded relations of gender and its intersections with class (poverty) may sometimes, not always, lead women to sex work. Moreover, there is no easy transfer of gender based interventions, such as those discussed above, to countries where sex and sexuality are taboo topics. Organized groups such as labor unions of sex workers or the facilitation of a movement of sex workers, as has been recently initiated in Southern India (called Taaras, meaning rapid progress), can become vehicles for raising awareness about sex work and sex workers as well as to challenge the violence they face.

3. *We recommend that national governments, international aid agencies, and NGOs invest resources for workshops and training programs of sex workers.* In addition to organizing sex workers, workshops, and training programs focused on resisting violence and understanding means and mechanisms for reporting violence can be empowering for sex workers. Such programs can also contribute to building the confidence of sex workers to challenge violence. Incorporating role plays with details for dealing with police can be useful for sex workers to understand laws and their rights. Expanding such efforts beyond covering a few (20–50) sex workers in a small town or semi-rural location will require adequate resources (funds)

from national governments and other international agencies. This recommendation is particularly important with home-based sex workers. These sex workers work within their homes and their identities often are not known to the public. Therefore, the organizers of these workshops should use multiple way to advertise and publicize the workshops and training programs in order to reach even sex workers who work behind closed doors.

4. *We call for the need to formulate laws that clarify the condition of sex workers and protect their rights.* The legal situation of sex work in many countries leaves sex workers particularly vulnerable to violence. Laws that govern sex work can be complicated and confusing, especially because laws are not uniform globally, or even within each country. Understanding the range of legislative and policy options for activists and enforcement agencies responses to sex work is critical to establishing policies consistent with respecting, protecting, and fulfilling the human rights of sex workers. Laws and policies on sex work should be based on the best available evidence about what works to protect health and civil, social, and legal rights. They should optimize sex workers' ability to realize the right to due process under the law, the right to privacy, the right to form associations, the right to be free of discrimination, abuse, and violence, and the right to work and to just and favorable conditions of work. Typically, sex work is prohibited in some settings and under some conditions, but allowed or tolerated in others. For example, it may be legal for one woman to sell sex from a property but illegal for multiple women to do so. Lacking civil rights means sex workers may be unable to complain about crimes against them. They may also be unable to enforce contracts, claim welfare, borrow money, or make civil claims in family and property matters in courts. This leaves many without redress against violence or exploitation. A better understanding of what laws there are and how they impact sex work is needed to conceptualize new and more effective legal and regulatory frameworks. International agencies such as the United Nations can pressure national governments to review legal and regulatory frameworks as related to the rights of sex workers and thereby reduce their experiences with violence. It is also necessary to ensure that the legal and regulatory framework is cognizant of all types of sex work and sex workers and does not employ a one-fits-all approach.

5. *There is a need for ensuring the enforcement of the laws and legal protections to ensure sex workers' access to justice.* Sex workers are vulnerable to

violence because of weak legal systems and the absence or weak enforcement mechanisms. Stigma prevents sex workers from benefiting from regulations, criminal law and anti–discrimination provisions that can protect other workers and people. It is well documented that criminalization and corrupt law enforcement force sex workers into "underground" spaces, impedes their willingness to test for HIV, and their ability to negotiate condom use. Confiscation of condoms by police and their use as evidence of prostitution are particularly clear examples of counterproductive and harmful enforcement. Sensitizing law enforcement agency personnel, such as the police, about sex work may enable the protection of sex workers' rights. Training programs can allow enforcement agencies to better assist sex workers to protect them from violence.

6. *We recommend that researchers who study violence against sex workers carefully consider methods for assessing effectiveness of programs aimed at addressing violence faced by sex workers.* If the goal of a researcher is to study violence faced by sex workers and recommend policy for mitigation of the violence, it would be appropriate to target a relatively large number of participants to provide information (and possible assistance) rather than a select few. It is vital that interventions be tailored to local conditions because what works well in one location may not be appropriate in another. Contextually relevant risk reduction interventions are therefore an important public policy priority. Large-scale epidemiological evidence is often considered over qualitative findings although both types of data are complementary and essential. The sole reliance on quantitative modes of analysis can render power relations, a key to examining violence, invisible. Efforts to adopt a mixed methods approach can be useful for gathering data that lends itself to analyze gendered power relations. Such an approach will allow for an assessment of the intangible benefits that accrue to sex workers.

7. *We argue that researchers should empower sex workers by utilizing the expertise and knowledge they have accumulated.* Tapping into the knowledge of sex workers and the strategies they adopt to cope with violence could be a first step in understanding what mechanisms may mitigate violence. Drawing on the intelligence of sex workers in how they handle conflicts and manage violence can also be useful for reducing risks to HIV. While most research studies and reports focus on much-needed details of types of violence and perpetrators of violence, it would be beneficial to understand how sex workers cope with violence.

8. *We recommend the support of "community" organizations of sex workers as they serve as support networks.* "Community" refers to the community of sex workers. Community organizing as related to sex workers can enable collective action to address structural barriers such as physical, social, cultural, and legal aspects of the environment that hinder efforts to mitigate violence. It involves initiating and building localized groups of sex workers and building their capacity to assume ownership of the community organization. Community organizations also provide sex workers with a channel for effective self-mobilization to access basic rights and services. Moreover, the organization serves as a support network and provides sex workers a space for sharing information about violence. Recognizing sex workers' community organizations as repositories of information can facilitate the replication and scaling-up of the accumulated expertise.

Key Citations

Decker, M., G.R. Seage III, D. Hemenway, A. Raj, N. Saggurti, D. Balaiah, and J.G. Silverman. (2009) Intimate partner violence functions as both a risk marker and risk factor for women's HIV infection: Findings from Indian husband-wife dyads, *Journal of Acquired Immune Deficiency Syndrome*, 51(5): 593-600.

Deering, K.N., A. Amin, J. Shoveller, A. Nesbitt, C. Garcia-Moreno, P. Duff, E. Argento, and K. Shannon. (2014) A systematic review of the correlates of violence against sex workers, *American Journal of Public Health*, 104(5): 42-54.

El-Bassel, N., S.S. Witte, L. Gilbert, E. Wu, M. Chang, J. Hill, and P. Steinglass. (2005) Long-term effects of an HIV/STI sexual risk reduction intervention for heterosexual couples, *AIDS and Behavior*, 9(1): 1-13.

Karandikar, S. and L.B. Gexinski. (2013) Intimate partner violence and HIV risks among female sex workers of Mumbai, India, *Journal of Ethnic & Cultural Diversity in Social Work*, 22:112-128.

Pronyk, P.M., J.R. Hargreaves, J.C. Kim, L.A. Morison, G. Phetla, C. Watts, J. Buza, and J.D.H. Porter. (2006) Effect of a structural intervention for the prevention of intimate-partner violence and HIV in rural South Africa: A cluster randomised trial, *Lancet*, 368(9551): 1973-1983.

Wingood, G.M. and R.J. DiClemente. (2000) Application of the theory of gender and power to examine HIV-related exposures, risk factors, and effective interventions for women, *Health Education & Behavior*, 27(5): 539-65.

World Health Organization. (2013) *16 Ideas for Addressing Violence Against Women in the Context of the HIV Epidemic.* Geneva, Switzerland: World Health Organization.

World Health Organization. (2005) *Violence Against Women and HIV/ AIDS: Critical Intersections- Violence Against Sex Workers and HIV Prevention.* Geneva, Switzerland: World Health Organization.

TWELVE

Genocide and other Atrocity Crimes: Toward Remedies[1]

Joachim J. Savelsberg, University of Minnesota

The Problem: Genocides and other Mass Atrocity Crimes

Throughout history, rulers and governments have committed mass killings and caused grave suffering to uncounted millions. Actors at all levels of hierarchy have been involved. Targets were their own subjects and citizens of other peoples and countries. Today, we refer to such acts of mass violence as mass atrocity crimes, a term coined by David Scheffer, formerly US Ambassador and aide to the Secretary of State Madeline Albright. The term encompasses genocide, crimes against humanity, and war crimes. In genocide, individuals are killed or harmed because they are members of a group (national, religious, racial, or ethnic), while crimes against humanity are systematic and widespread attacks directed against civilian populations regardless of their group membership. War crimes are action carried out during the conduct of a war that breaches accepted international rules of war. International treaties provide legal definitions, especially the Convention on the Prevention and Punishment of the Crime of Genocide of 1948 or the Rome Statute of 1998, the foundation of the International Criminal Court.

Some scholars use modified terms to evade the limitations for legal definitions. Political scientist R.J. Rummel, for example, writes about democide (murder of peoples by a government, including genocide), politicide (murder of groups because of their politics or for political purposes), and mass murder (indiscriminate killing). Rummel estimates the death toll at 169.202 million for the period 1900 to 1987 (not

---

[1] The author thanks Alejandro Baer, Brooke Chambers, and the editors for carefully reading the text and for suggestions toward improvement.

including victims of "legitimate" warfare). The number of victims of murder, manslaughter, and homicide in civil society during the same period amounts to only about ten percent of this death count (see the author's *Crime and Human Rights*). In addition to killings, mass atrocity crimes typically involve mass rapes, destruction of livelihood, and displacements of entire populations.

Despite great variation concerning the methods of killings, the execution of mass atrocity crimes in times of peace versus war, and the number of victims, there are also commonalities. All involve collective action, complex social organization, often including formal organizations, with front-line, low-level actors who execute the dirty work, as well as high-level actors whose hands remain untainted by the blood for the shedding of which they bear ultimate responsibility. Many constitute organizational crimes. Yet, at times, actors also seek to satisfy their own greed or sadistic desires—independent of, or even disadvantageous to, the organization's goals. After legal innovations of the 20th and 21st centuries, all of these transgressions legally constitute crimes. Many were committed in disregard of domestic law and all of them constitute crimes according to international humanitarian and human rights laws, the beginnings of which reach back to the 19th century, and the development of which accelerated after World War II and the Holocaust and, again, toward the end of the 20th century.

Research Evidence

Conditions of Genocide and other Atrocity Crimes

Mass atrocity crimes are most likely to unfold in places and eras in which systems of domestic or international checks and balances are missing. Desensitization toward violence and chaos in the context of war are further risk factors. Periods of heightened risk are thus times of dictatorship and/or war. Democracy and peace are the best safeguards against war crimes, crimes against humanity, and genocide. Another crucial precursor of mass atrocity crimes is the systematic dehumanization of ethnic, racial, religious, or other minority groups, and, more generally, the construction of group boundaries, practices of "othering" by means of bolstering cultural and political differences within societies.

Current scholarship focuses on such risk factors, triggers, and escalating dynamics, and on individual perpetrators. A recent publication by the United States Holocaust Memorial Museum, authored by political scientist Scott Strauss, provides a summary. Sophisticated analyses examine patterns by which structural conditions and political initiatives evoke motivation at the level of individual actors that accelerates through use of hate-filled language and rituals within social groups to result in the execution of genocide. Work by sociologist-criminologists John Hagan and Wenona Rymond-Richmond on Darfur provides an excellent example.

Definition of Mass Atrocities as a Social Problem

For much of human history, those responsible for mass killings were celebrated as heroes and great state builders. Such attitudes began to change only in the 19th century, with the promulgation of legal norms and institutions, first against the slave trade and later against war crimes, the latter articulated in the Hague and Geneva Conventions. Change accelerated in the aftermath of World War II and the Holocaust. Criminal justice played an increasingly central role in such responses. Documenting the substantial increase in prosecutions against suspected perpetrators of human rights crimes, political scientist Kathryn Sikkink describes the late 20th and early 21st centuries as an era of a justice cascade.

Yet, criminal justice, from domestic to international systems, is only part of a broad repertoire of responses. Other institutional responses may supplement it or take its place. They include truth (and reconciliation) commissions, compensation payments, lustration (the banning of categories of people, such as members of the previous ruling party, from government jobs), public apologies by government officials, and the establishment of memorials and commemorative rituals.

Driving forces of such change include evolving cultural sensitivities, a new stress on the dignity of the individual, which classical sociologist Émile Durkheim described powerfully in his response to the Dreyfus Affair in his native France. Structural forces include an intensification of economic, cultural, and political ties that create mutual dependencies across nations, and the building of international organizations, most noteworthy of these the United Nations. Political scientists Margaret Keck and Kathryn Sikkink have highlighted the role of international non-governmental organizations, often linked into Trans-National Activist networks (TANs). Such TANs engage in *information politics* that tie networks together in attempts to affect political actors; *symbolic and leverage politics* to mobilize shame against powerful corporations or governments; and *accountability politics*, seeking to convince governments to change their rhetoric on an issue, and, once successful, to hold them accountable. In short, social problem and penal entrepreneurs played a crucial role in defining mass atrocities as a social problem and those involved as criminal perpetrators, but they could succeed only in the context of shifting cultural and structural conditions.

In short, and in line with an argument first articulated by Harvard jurist Martha Minow, earlier eras may well compete with the 20th century in terms of the intensity of mass atrocities; yet the 20th century is unique, as humankind attempted for the first time to respond with systematic policy responses. Actors in world society defined mass atrocities as a major social problem and those who initiate or execute them as criminal perpetrators. They began to build institutions aimed at preventing, or responding to, mass atrocity crimes.

Despite such institutional change, many cases, including some of the gravest, still unfold without responses, partly because of immense power imbalances in international relations. In addition, individual and collective denial is still common, a tendency that may in fact have intensified in response to the successful criminalization of mass atrocities. Criminologist Stanley Cohen distinguished three types of denial: factual (it did not happen); interpretive (what happened was something different); and implicatory (it happened, but I was not part of it).

Recommendations and Solutions

Given the complexity of mass atrocities, and the conditions under which they unfold, solutions are either hard to achieve or complex, with various side effects, some unintended and potentially counterproductive consequences. There are no easy solutions, but the following paragraphs outline suggestions, supporting them with evidence from recent research. Given ongoing debates, I first state each recommendation, followed by reasoning and supportive evidence.

Checks and balances: democracy

Recommendation: Strengthen democratic regimes and systems of domestic checks and balances. **Reasoning**: As mass atrocities commonly unfold under conditions of massive power concentration, the establishment and maintenance of systems of checks and balances is possibly the most effective protector against mass atrocity crimes.

Peace and the absence of war

Recommendation: Seek to avoid war. **Reasoning**: Even democracies, when they engage in warfare, run the risk of engaging in, encouraging, or enabling mass atrocity crimes. Often the boundary between militarily necessary and legitimate strategies and criminal violence is blurry, as illustrated by debates over bombing campaigns on civilian targets in many modern wars, and the nuclear bombs on Hiroshima and Nagasaki. Further, war tends to be associated with the dehumanization of the enemy people, thereby inviting mass atrocities. Finally, the daily experience of violence and death lowers the bar for military personnel to engage in violence and killings beyond the boundaries defined by the laws of war (Geneva Conventions).

Criminal law

Penal responses to mass atrocity crimes likely reduce the risk of their recurrence. Domestic and international institutions may be involved.

Domestic criminal law

Recommendation: Strengthen the capacity of domestic courts to respond to atrocity crimes. **Reasoning**: Domestic criminal court responses are best suited in transitional justice situations, after periods of civil war and dictatorship (e.g., Greece and Argentina after military dictatorships). In addition to fulfilling a retributive function, they may also deter political and military leaders from engaging in grave human rights violations. Analyses by Kathryn Sikkink and her collaborators indicate potential, albeit slight, improvements of human rights records after criminal prosecutions of perpetrators. Improvements are enhanced when truth commissions accompany court responses (below).

International criminal law

Recommendation: Strengthen the capacity of international human rights courts. **Reasoning**: International criminal justice responses are indicated when domestic courts are not capable or not willing to prosecute. The aftermath of World War II witnessed international criminal justice institutions in Germany and Japan. After a hiatus during the Cold War, international or hybrid (mixed national–international) tribunals in the 1990s responded to mass atrocities; for example, in the cases of the former Yugoslavia, Rwanda, Cambodia, and East Timor.

While some scholars, such as Max Pensky, Jack Snyder, or Leslie Vinjamuri, doubt the benefits of international prosecution, recent research by Hyeran Jo and Beth Simmons shows that International Criminal Court prosecutions in fact result in a decline in mass atrocities committed by government and by rebel groups alike. This work, like that of Kathryn Sikkink, has focused on the deterrence effect of criminal prosecution.

Enhancing cultural effects of criminal prosecution

Recommendation: Enhance the cultural power of criminal prosecution against perpetrators of human rights violations. **Reasoning**: Effects of (international) prosecution are not limited to deterrence, based on assumptions of rational actors. Recent work instead highlights the representational power of courts, their chance to impress on a global public, even against resistance, an understanding of mass violence as a form of criminal violence. Such potential may turn into symbolic power à la Pierre Bourdieu. The author's own work on collective representations of the mass violence in the Darfur region of Sudan and his related work, with Ryan D. King, on the ICTY and the My Lai trial provides empirical evidence of such cultural effects. Sources of the strength of criminal courts in the realm of culture include their ritual power, access to channels of communication (communicative power), and authority based on procedurally based legitimacy. Once judicial representations have generated memories, these memories unfold their own normative force, as Daniel Levy and Natan Sznaider have documented in their historical comparative work. Effective methods of communication between courts and media as well as the spheres of education, cultural production and the arts must be developed to enhance the cultural effect of criminal trials against human rights perpetrators. Research by this author points at some impediments and opportunities to advance such communication.

Limitations of criminal prosecutions

Recommendation: Enhance awareness of limitations of prosecutions. **Reasoning**: Criminal justice representations are constrained by a specific institutional logic, resulting in a narrow account of atrocities. They operate with a simplifying binary logic of guilty versus not guilty, leaving out shades of grey, which are essential to fully grasp the causes, unfolding, and implications of the crimes. They focus on the role of individual actors rather than structural forces and broader cultural patterns that sociologists would consider. They are constrained by legal categories under which responsible actors such as cultural enablers of genocide and bystanders cannot be subsumed. They are further limited by evidentiary rules that exclude evidence that historians and social scientists would take seriously. These constraints suggest that criminal prosecutions be accompanied by supplemental mechanisms.

Truth commissions and other transitional justice mechanisms

Recommendation: Supplement trials by truth commissions (TC). **Reasoning**: Truth commissions are one supplemental mechanism. A detailed comparative analysis by Priscilla Hayner suggests potential benefits under specific circumstances, while also clarifying the variable relationship between criminal justice and truth commissions. In El Salvador, the TC report prompted a general amnesty. Like in Argentina, TCs in Uganda and Haiti produced evidence that supported later prosecutions. In Chile, the TC worked under an amnesty law that was already in place; but its work later strengthened international prosecutions. Only in South Africa was the TRC authorized to offer amnesties to specific perpetrators. Where TCs are not accompanied or followed by trials, supporters argue, is in settings with little hope for effective prosecution in the first place, due to economic constraints, lack of training, corrupt "justice" systems, or the continuing influence of past perpetrators on criminal courts.

Importantly, TCs have contributed to accountability in ways not available to criminal courts. For example, instead of attributing responsibility to particular individuals alone, they are better suited to examine broader patterns of abuses, thereby encouraging institutional reforms. They thus also challenge broad sectors of society and segments of the population that carry some degree of responsibility, from bureaucrats to torturers and profiteers all the way to by-standers who refused to speak up. Yet, the work of TCs faces limits as well. Critics stress that TCs are more concerned with collective well-being than with the fate of individuals.

Bridges and overlaps between contending social fields

Recommendation: Enhance communication across benevolent social fields. **Reasoning**: Research conducted by this author has shown that zero-sum assumptions about conflicting cultural representations of mass violence between competing benevolent social fields at times block potential for collaboration. Examples are human rights NGOs that pursue justice narratives, humanitarian organizations—in need for permits by the perpetrating state—that speak in terms of humanitarian emergencies, and foreign policy makers—under the pressure to negotiate—who prefer the language of armed conflict. My research on Darfur has shown that zero-sum assumptions be questioned and that room for collaboration should and can be explored.

Responsibility to Protect (R2P)

Recommendation: Strengthen R2P. **Reasoning**: While trials and truth commission respond to mass atrocities, other strategies seek to prevent them or interfere in their unfolding. The "Responsibility to protect populations from genocide, war crimes, ethnic cleansing and crimes against humanity," codified in paragraphs 138 and 139 of the UN General Assembly Resolution of September 16, 2005, is one such strategy. Paragraph 138 establishes the responsibility of States to protect their populations from genocide, war crimes, ethnic cleansing and crimes against humanity; paragraph 139 elaborates on the responsibility of the international community.

While so-called Realists stress that the doctrine evokes counterproductive interventions and is naïve in presuming that States are guided by moral considerations, the juxtaposition of interests and moral appeal is artificial. Countries recognize that adherence to international norms shapes their image and that such an image plays to their interest. Critics also point at limits of enforcement and accountability. Indeed, countries are tempted to take a free rider position when the protection of populations is at stake. Solutions, developed by Jean-Baptiste Jeangène Villmer, include assigning responsibility for specific cases to specific states (e.g., Australia toward East Timor) and the task of distribution to specific institutions (e.g., UNSC). Arguments against anti-imperialism critique that R2P serves as a Trojan horse of post-colonial domination include these objections: the occident is far from homogeneous when interventions are at stake; interventions typically do not lead to long-term occupation; and interventionist tendencies are substantial even in parts of the Global South, especially Africa.

A successful implementation of R2P would diminish the risk of the despair and helplessness experienced, for example, by the Dutch UN military forces in Srebrenica and, on a yet incomparably larger scale by Roméo Dallaire, commander of UN troops in Rwanda during the genocide. Not provided with the forces and not given adequate authority, he was unable to prevent the killings of hundreds of thousands.

The issue of climate change

Recommendation: Control climate change that devastates livelihoods. **Reasoning**: Climate change enhances conflicts over tightening natural resources. Desertification in North Africa is a troubling example. It intensifies conflicts between nomadic and pastoral peoples and carries the risk of mass violence where political forces exploit these conflicts.

Early warning systems

Recommendation: Create early warning systems. **Reasoning**: Governments and international organizations have invested heavily into early warning systems for natural catastrophes. Similar efforts for human made events such as genocides are only in their infancy. Yet, social science has the potential to develop prognostic tools that would allow recognizing the risk of mass atrocities and enhancing chances of early intervention.

Key Resources

Hagan, J. and Rymond-Richmond, W. (2009) *Darfur and the Crime of Genocide*, Cambridge/New York: Cambridge University Press.

Hayner, P. *Unspeakable Truths: Transitional Justice and the Challenge of Truth Commissions*, 2nd edn, London: Routledge.

Hyeran, J. and Simmons, B. (2016) Can the International Criminal Court Deter Atrocity?, *International Organization* 70/3:443–475.

Rummel, R.J. (1994) *Death by Government*, New Brunswick, NJ: Transaction.

Rymond-Richmond, W. (2013) *The Criminology of Genocide. Oxford Bibliographies online*, www.oxfordbibliographies.com/view/document/obo-9780195396607/obo-9780195396607-0159.xml

Savelsberg, J.J. (2015) *Representing Mass Violence: Collective Responses to Human Rights Violations in Darfur.* Oakland: University of California Press.

Savelsberg, J.J. and King, R.D. (2011) *American Memories: Atrocities and the Law*, New York: Russell Sage Foundation.

Sikkink, K. (2011) *Justice Cascade: How Human Rights Prosecutions are Changing World Politics*, New York: Norton.

Straus, S. (2016) *Fundamentals of Genocide and Mass Atrocity Prevention*, Washington, DC: United States Holocaust Memorial Museum.

Vilmer, J-B. J. (2015) *La Responsabilité de Protéger*. Paris: Presses Universitaires de France.

THIRTEEN

Torture: Causes, Consequences, and Strategies for Redress and Prevention

Shannon Golden, The Center for Victims of Torture

The Problem

Until relatively recent history, torture was regarded as a necessary practice for legal or state control. Moves to abolish the use of torture began in the late 18th century and began to lay the groundwork for the principle that all humans have basic rights that must be respected by states. With the rise of international human rights norms, laws, institutions, and activism in the 20th century, the right to freedom from torture became regarded as one of the most fundamental human rights. Definitions of torture are now codified in national and transnational agreements, notably the United Nations Convention Against Torture (UNCAT). Some national legislation mirrors inclusive language found in the UNCAT definition, while other countries have more narrowly focused definitions of torture. According to UNCAT, torture is any act—outside of lawful sanctions—that intentionally inflicts severe physical or mental suffering, perpetrated by or with the acquiescence of someone in authority, to gain information, force a confession, punish, intimidate, coerce, or discriminate. Torture can be perpetrated by formal, state-based authorities, such as police or military, or by *de facto* authorities, such as armed groups controlling territory. Despite such definitions, identifying torture can be complex and ambiguous in practice, as legal definitions can be difficult to apply to complex social situations.

Furthermore, even when definitions are clear, moral ambiguity can remain. Despite near-universal condemnation of torture in principle, as a fundamental violation of human rights and dignity, throughout the 20th century, and now well into the 21st, democratic justifications for the use of torture have persisted. For example, as modern warfare becomes more asymmetric, even regimes with rights-respecting rhetoric at times justify the use of torture as necessary to protect national security. Other states may publicly adopt anti-torture agreements to gain international legitimacy and deflect attention from continued abuses. This complex history and current landscape illustrate how torture as a social problem is continually constructed and contested.

Despite efforts to curtail its use and hold perpetrators accountable, torture occurs with alarming regularity and remains a pressing contemporary global social problem. Specific instances and patterns of torture are documented by a range of human rights organizations, other civil society actors, as well as governmental or intergovernmental authorities. We know that torture occurs, but establishing global prevalence estimates is exceptionally difficult, as the practice remains hidden by those in power, violations are underreported due to fear and stigma, and torture can result in victims' death. We have evidence for the prevalence of torture in specific contexts or among particular sub-populations, such as among help-seeking populations or among refugee populations in camps or in countries of resettlement. Among populations seeking help from service providers or among asylum-seeking arrivals in countries of refuge, estimated rates of torture prevalence can be exceptionally high. Prevalence estimates can vary widely, as data are rarely collected from representative samples, populations are very diverse, and torture is difficult to assess reliably. Despite challenges in collecting this data, the evidence we do have reveals a social problem of disturbing magnitude.

Research Evidence

Evidence helps us to understand many dimensions of torture, although some areas remain in need of increased research attention. There is substantial evidence about what is wrong with torture. For example, while there is evidence that torture is ineffective in meeting its purported goals, such as producing reliable information, it can be highly effective in spreading fear and terror among populations. There is a significant body of research focused on the negative consequences of torture on victims, including often chronic, multidimensional physical and psychological effects (e.g., psychiatric diagnoses, PTSD), and negative social impacts on families, communities, and societies, some lasting for multiple generations. There is evidence that perpetrators also experience negative mental health effects, at times severe. With the growth of a global movement against torture, specialized interventions are now available for torture survivors, leading to a substantial body of research focused on the efficacy of rehabilitation services for torture survivors, particularly focused on mental health interventions.

Research on the causes of torture focus on two distinct but interrelated levels of explanation. First, there are analyses of how and why torture emerges and persists in particular social, cultural, political, and legal contexts. This includes the use of torture to control, discriminate against, or punish segments of populations, to pursue national security goals, to spread terror, and so on. Second, there is research focused on more proximal causes of torture, emerging from interpersonal interactions and social exchange between torturer and tortured. These analyses advance understanding of how and why individuals commit seemingly inconceivable atrocities, including now well-known studies on obedience to authority. At this level, analyses can include the social groups, histories, beliefs, values, politics, and organizations in which individuals are embedded.

Research also helps us understand the rise and efficacy of the global movement against torture. Macro-level studies on the global diffusion of the anti-torture movement analyze when, where, and how international norms spread (or do not spread) to diverse national contexts, such as through states ratifying international treaties, the passage of domestic legislation, or by the growth of national human rights organizations. There is also research about how transnational advocacy networks emerge around human rights issues in attempts to hold governments accountable to their commitments. Torture is an issue well suited for highly effective transnational advocacy, due to the fact that it involves physical harms perpetrated against vulnerable individuals. Additionally, transitional justice and criminal justice research explores in what circumstances individuals or groups can be held accountable for acts of torture, and what the consequences of these justice efforts are for perpetrators, survivors, and societies more broadly.

Finally, there is some evidence about public knowledge of and opinions about torture. Public opinion helps us understand how and when torture is regarded as legitimate or how to mobilize publics to hold governments accountable. This is highly salient in the contemporary political moment, particularly in the United States, as torture is framed as a divisive moral issue, at times a necessary trade-off to ensure national security. Public opinion data can reveal in what circumstances ordinary citizens support the use of torture and what types of people are more likely to see torture as permissible or necessary.

Recommendations and Solutions

Solutions for the global problem of torture can focus on advancing two goals: 1) to realize the right to redress for victims of torture; and 2) to realize the right to freedom from torture. Both of these areas require survivor involvement, public engagement, and a multi-level approach. First, survivors must be engaged in imagining and implementing solutions. Torture fundamentally strips people of their basic human dignity; involving survivors in creating strategies to promote healing and prevent torture is a way of restoring dignity, as well as helping to develop solutions that are meaningful and viable. Second, public education and awareness-raising is a necessary step to advance both of these areas. Far-reaching campaigns in the global public sphere must increase awareness of what torture is and frame it unequivocally as a violation of human rights in all circumstances. Awareness campaigns should also focus on the fact that receiving redress after torture is also a human right protected by international law. Third, solutions to advance both redress and prevention must consider both individual and collective levels of strategic intervention. Torture harms individuals and social groups, so the most effective solutions must strategically integrate multi-level approaches.

In addition to defining and prohibiting torture, the UNCAT enshrines victims' right to redress in international law. Redress means providing remedy and repair for the harms caused by torture and includes victims' rights to: restitution, compensation, rehabilitation, satisfaction, and guarantee of non-repetition. Victims include individuals and collectives who directly or indirectly suffered harms from torture. States ultimately have responsibility to realize victims' right to redress, but in practice, most services are provided by non-state actors. Pressure must be put on states to fulfill their obligations, whether by providing services directly or by increasing funding available to medical facilities or NGOs. States can be pressured to increase voluntary contributions to the United Nations Voluntary Fund for Victims of Torture, which provides humanitarian assistance to victims; contributions are low, relative to need, and key contributors have discussed reducing their contributions even further. To fully realize the right to redress, there is a need for substantial increase in resources.

Redress for victims or survivors must include socioeconomic support and other programs focused on making restitution (that is, restoring the state of living prior to torture). In practice, complete restitution is rarely possible, as many survivors have fled their home countries and completely lost most or all elements of their previous life, including homes, livelihoods, educational or career opportunities. Despite these challenges, a holistic approach to individual and collective restitution should address the structural causes or factors that contributed to the violation (such as discrimination), and promote refugee and asylum policies that are oriented towards restoration of dignity.

For many survivors of torture, rehabilitation from the trauma of what they endured requires specialized, interdisciplinary clinical services, such as psychotherapy or physiotherapy. To effectively meet the needs of torture survivors, service providers should use evidence-based interventions and strengthen research initiatives to understand the impact of different interventions with different populations (e.g., for children and adolescents, or across religious and cultural groups). This area would benefit from a deepened integration of research and service provision. Advancing research in this area would help identify best practices in meeting very specific needs of torture survivors and in responsibly utilizing resources allotted. This should include more holistic conceptualizations of rehabilitation outcomes (beyond PTSD, anxiety, etc.) to include social or collective impacts. Another necessity is to increase access to available rehabilitation services. This includes: expanding services to a fuller range of locations; campaigns to decrease stigma around receiving services; and efforts to provide protections for those fearful of receiving services.

Providing survivors with satisfaction for the violations they endured includes advocating for and promoting judicial accountability, acknowledgment or apology, and survivors' right to the truth about what happened. Holistic healing and rehabilitation, for some survivors, requires participation in justice initiatives; to facilitate this, truth-telling, accountability, and reconciliation mechanisms should prioritize trauma-sensitive inclusion of survivors. In other cases, truth commissions, memorialization activities, or criminal trials may not benefit individuals, but may provide redress for collective victims by advancing accountability for past wrongs and contributing to deterrence of future violations.

The second goal is to realize the right to freedom from torture, or to abolish the use of torture around the world. Torture is one of the few human rights violations that is universally condemned in international law (in any and all circumstances), as well as in much legislation. For governments that have not ratified the UNCAT or enacted domestic legislation prohibiting torture, that must be the first strategic target for anti-torture advocates. A key mechanism to realize freedom from torture is to leverage rhetorical and legal commitments that states have already made to not using torture. This includes advocacy at the transnational level, particularly within the United Nations system. This also includes the development and support of strong national human rights and advocacy sectors capable of directly holding governments to account, or using indirect channels available through transnational advocacy networks. Strategies include: holding governments accountable through public naming and shaming campaigns; rigorous collection of evidence and documenting incidences and patterns of torture; pursuing criminal prosecutions for individuals directly responsible; and presenting evidence to UN treaty bodies and the Human Rights Council.

Protecting people from torture also requires a more micro-level strategy to address proximal, interpersonal, or institutional causes of torture. Providing consistent training on human rights principles and practices for all range of security sector actors (military, police, etc.) may aid in preventing torture. Sufficiently resourcing police and prison systems can decrease the likelihood that officers will resort to torture. Courts that prosecute individuals for torture may provide a deterrence effect to prevent specific individuals from committing abuse. Increasing the level of institutional oversight of military and security forces, of practices in detention facilities, and of judicial proceedings may decrease systematic patterns of abuse.

Across these areas, key obstacles to abolishing the practice of torture and in providing redress for survivors include: inadequate legislation; lack of acknowledgement by states; lack of resources; and inaccessible systems of redress, due to discrimination, stigma, culture, language, proximity, and vulnerability. Strategies to overcome such obstacles must focus on: mobilizing financial resources (such as through pressuring states to fulfill their obligations); raising public awareness of the continuance of torture; involving survivors in designing strategies; lobbying for more enforceable legislation; activating transnational advocacy networks to hold rights-violating states accountable; strengthening courts and other mechanisms to handle complaints and conduct investigations; and building the capacity of service providers to deliver effective rehabilitation services. Torture is an issue with nearly universal condemnation, demonstrating the success of previous eras of transnational and domestic organizing and advocacy to address a pressing social problem. This international consensus now provides a powerful springboard to build upon and propel us firmly into an era in which there are no longer victims of torture.

Key References

Amnesty International (2018) Amnesty International Report 2017/18: The State of the World's Human Rights. London: Amnesty International. Available at: www.amnesty.org/en/documents/POL10/6700/2018/En/. Last accessed March 22, 2018.

Barnes, J. (2017) *A Genealogy of the Torture Taboo*. New York: Routledge.

Costanzo, M.A. and Gerrity, E. (2009) The Effects and Effectiveness of Using Torture as an Interrogation Device: Using Research to Inform the Policy Debate, *Social Issues and Policy Review*, 3(1): 179–210.

Gross, M.L. (2010) *Moral Dilemmas of Modern War: Torture, Assassination, and Blackmail in an Age of Asymmetric Conflict*. Cambridge: Cambridge University Press.

Hajjar, L. (2009) Does Torture Work? A Sociolegal Assessment of the Practice in Historical and Global Perspective, *Annual Review of Law and Social Science*, 5: 311–45.

Hajjar, L. (2013) *Torture: A Sociology of Violence and Human Rights*. New York: Routledge.

Kalt, A., Hossain, M., Kiss, L. and Zimmerman, C. (2013) Asylum Seekers, Violence and Health: A Systematic Review of Research in High-Income Host Countries. *American Journal of Public Health*, 103(3): e30–42.

Steel, Z., Chey, T., Silove, D., Marnane, C., Bryant, R.A. and van Ommeren, M. (2009) Association of Torture and Other Potentially Traumatic Events with Mental Health Outcomes among Populations Exposed to Mass Conflict and Displacement: A Systematic Review and Meta-Analysis, *JAMA*, 302(5): 537–49.

Vreeland, J.R. (2008) Political Institutions and Human Rights: Why Dictatorships Enter into the United Nations Convention Against Torture, *International Organization*, 62(1): 65–101.

Weiss, W.M., Ugueto, SA.M., Mahmooth, Z., Murray, L.K., Hall, B.J., Nadison, M., Rasmussen, R. et al (2016) Mental Health Interventions and Priorities for Research for Adult Survivors of Torture and Systematic Violence: A Review of the Literature, *Torture*, 26(1): 17–44.

Key organizations and networks for further engagement:

World Organization Against Torture (OMCT) www.omct.org

Convention Against Torture Initiative (CTI) www.cti2024.org

Association for the Prevention of Torture (APT) www.apt.ch

International Rehabilitation Council for Torture Victims (IRCT) www.irct.org

SECTION V

Inequalities and Disparities

FOURTEEN

Want Amidst Plenty: Food Insecurity in Rich Liberal Democracies

David Reynolds and Miranda Mirosa

This chapter is about food insecurity, a social problem common across rich liberal democracies. In these countries, food insecurity and hunger are thought of as problems located overseas—surrounded by landscapes scarred by drought or battered by civil war. Countries populated with supermarket aisles brimming with foodstuffs and pizza delivery services are clearly not food insecure. And it's true: rich liberal democracies are not food insecure countries. Yet the United States of America, Canada, the United Kingdom, Australia and New Zealand all share a persistent trend—that a significant minority of their populations suffer food insecurity. A broadly accepted definition is that:

- food security exists when there is access by all people at all times to enough food for an active, healthy life, where there is at a minimum:

  a) the ready availability of nutritionally adequate and safe foods, and
  b) the assured ability to acquire acceptable foods in socially acceptable ways.

Year after year households in wealthy societies, despite being surrounded by readily available and safe foodstuffs, suffer food insecurity.

The Problem

In some areas, the readily available foods are not nutritionally adequate. These are often called "food deserts." In many more places, nutritionally adequate foods are *available*, but are not *accessible* by those households which are unable to buy them. In rich liberal democracies, the normal and socially acceptable way to acquire food is to purchase it. If a household cannot buy enough food, it is food insecure. If a household does have enough food but someone had to visit a food bank (food pantry), a dumpster, or a community kitchen to get that food, it is food insecure. A household is also food insecure if they are not confident that they will be able to get enough nutritious food in the near future. These criteria may appear to offer a low bar for qualification as food insecure, but it is not unreasonable to expect that citizens in rich liberal democracies should be able to live without the fear that they will be unable to get enough nutritious food to eat. A portion of the population in "first-world" countries brimming with food should not consistently have difficulty in accessing food.

Food insecurity is a social problem because enough food is *available* but it is not *accessible* by all. That is, the problem is one of distribution rather than availability—of want despite plenty. It is also a political problem because particular groups of people disproportionately suffer food insecurity, in trends persistent across time and internationally across rich liberal democracies. Food insecurity is also a health problem, with significant detrimental consequences for the health of individuals who suffer it. The popular imagination of food insecurity as a problem "over there" exists for a reason: rich liberal democracies do have plenty of food. Food insecurity in these countries is all the more shameful for being surrounded by plenty, and all the more disturbing because it is a persistent social condition suffered by a significant minority of the population.

Research Evidence

There are three types of research evidence concerning food insecurity—evidence about its outcomes, about its incidence, and about its causes and associated factors.

What we know about the health outcomes of food insecurity provides clear cause for concern about this social problem. We know that for children, food insecurity impairs physical and mental development. It is a factor in their development of obesity, behavioral problems, chronic illnesses, and health problems leading to hospitalization, and it impedes positive educational outcomes. We know that adults who suffer food insecurity have nutrient deficiencies, are more likely to be obese, to develop type 2 diabetes, heart disease, and high blood pressure. They are more likely to suffer multiple chronic conditions and major depression and distress, and to have poorer mental and physical health generally.

We know that the incidence food insecurity was not a concern for the decades following the Depression of the 1930s; food was widely available and broadly accessible, with the exception of war-time national shortages which necessitated food rationing systems. The problem re-emerged in rich liberal democracies as neoliberal rationality developed significant influence in the early 1980s. In particular, the notions of "small government" and individualism shaped public policies, the operation of political economies, and the orientation of public debate, with significant consequences for life in these societies. This rationality was paired with the development of policy based on conservative values under Reagan in the USA, Thatcher in the UK, and Mulroney in Canada. These "New Right" governments rolled back social security protections, unravelling social safety nets for the most vulnerable, and promoted rhetoric which framed those suffering food insecurity, as well as poverty and long-term unemployment, as being at fault for their predicaments.

What we know about the incidence of food insecurity in rich liberal democracies varies by the data produced for each country. The USA and Canada have collected and released nationally representative data annually since 1995, while the UK began biennial data collection in 2010. Similar quality data for Australia and New Zealand are patchy. All countries have data collected and released by emergency food provision charities or groups of charities, which may well be indicative of trends, but often lacks a rigorous collection methodology. While the data available varies, what is common between these countries is the disturbing level of incidence, given both the availability of food and the existence of structures at least nominally intended to support their most vulnerable people.

The data available from each of these countries shows that the incidence of food insecurity rarely falls below 10% for the general population and is consistently far higher for particular groups of people. Research evidence shows clearly that insufficient household income is the primary reason for households to be food insecure. However, poverty is not the sole cause of food insecurity. There are several demographic categories notable for the consistency of their association with food insecurity across time and across countries. These are: "low income" for household income level; "female" for gender; "Indigenous" or "minority" for ethnicity; and "sole-parent" (especially female-headed) for household structure. The consistency of these categories indicates the systemic nature of significant drivers of food insecurity in rich liberal democracies. This situation calls for urgent policy action to engage with these systems, the detrimental effects they produce, and the positions of citizens within them.

Recommendations and Solutions

The remainder of this chapter is oriented towards discussing policy recommendations to address a social problem: the persistent levels of food insecurity across rich liberal democracies. The research evidence supports a focus on structural drivers of food insecurity in this discussion of solutions. *Social* problems are problems which people encounter, or do not encounter, largely depending on their membership of *social* groups. A complex set of dynamics generate the social problem of food insecurity, but there is evidence that structures make up the substantial and underlying drivers.

Research evidence shows that several of these social groups (described above) are consistent internationally and across decades. It is not the poor choices or lifestyles of individuals which create trends of social problems at the level of social groups, but rather the influence of structures on populations. Two pieces of evidence in particular support the idea that food insecurity is a social problem generated by structures similar across time and countries: the consistent primacy of insufficient income as a driver of food insecurity, and the consistency of the social groups that disproportionately suffer food insecurity. The evidence highlights the structures of political economy, but also flags the influence of social structures—gender, ethnicity, family structure. These structures overlap and interact with how people experience life in a political economy.

The policy measures described here address structures which are linked to food insecurity. Policy measures are an attractive way of addressing the structural roots of social problems because policies can inform and affect the form and operation of structures—in this case, the international incidence of food insecurity among certain social groups, across rich liberal democracies. To provide a foundation for this discussion of policy solutions, we introduce the concept of *vulnerability* and offer some observations about the need for policy action, its context and its intent. Then we describe some policy options which aim to alter the conditions or outcomes of the systems in which people live, or to cultivate peoples' own capacity to remain food secure. Finally, we offer some evaluation of policies in terms of broad political context.

Describing need: the concept of vulnerability

The research evidence available describes factors associated with suffering food insecurity, showing that: (1) insufficient income is consistently the primary factor driving food insecurity; and (2) there are particular groups in the populations of rich liberal democracies who are consistently much more vulnerable to food insecurity than other groups. The concept of vulnerability accommodates both the evidence that insufficient income is the primary driver of food insecurity, and the evidence that there are multiple other factors clearly associated with suffering food insecurity. It also explains the way that households suffer food insecurity—in the year in which they are measured as having been food insecure, the majority of households are not food insecure for the entirety, or even most of the year: they are scraping by, maintaining food security through scrupulous budgeting and making-do. Approaching solutions to food insecurity using the lens of vulnerability also brings into focus specific and practically oriented responses—effective responses to food insecurity are those which reduce vulnerability to food insecurity.

Structures and values: context and the need for policy

Before recommending specific policy measures, we describe three vital dynamics in the context of food insecurity in rich liberal democracies. We do this to provide some background understanding of some elements in the context of the social problem, which inform the focus of the policy recommendations. The first dynamic has already been raised: the operation of forms of neoliberal political economy in these countries, which is informed by the influence of neoliberal rationality on policy making. Focussing on households' ability to access food, it is apparent that neoliberal and neoconservative policies have shaped political economies across rich liberal democracies to make many households vulnerable to food insecurity. This disproportionately affects certain social groups, which makes these groups disproportionately vulnerable to food insecurity.

As well as influencing policy, neoliberal rationality also highlights the contributions which individual characteristics—vices or "lifestyle choices"—can make to a household being vulnerable to food insecurity. While such things as gambling or substance abuse can certainly be a problem for individual households, research evidence makes it clear that in general they are minor contributors to the incidence of food

135

insecurity. Food insecurity afflicts social groups, so that policy actions are viable and necessary responses to address this social problem: a problem of access, not availability; a problem for disadvantaged groups of people, not of deviant individuals.

A second dynamic which is important in the context of social problem and policy solution is the "elasticity" of a household's food budget. Some demands on a household's budget are inelastic, such as housing or electricity; these payments cannot be reduced by a few dollars to help a household to meet another cost. A household's food budget is elastic because it is possible to spend less on food in a given week to meet a cost. This means that a household's access to food can be impinged upon by any number of stresses—food, fuel, or housing costs rising faster than wages; an unexpected medical bill, car tyre replacement, or bank fee. A household is vulnerable to food insecurity where getting by week to week employs cost-saving measures and making do to the point that, when some crisis arrives, an already stretched food budget is the only elastic resource available to support a response. While food is a priority for households, circumstances and the budget's elasticity link food security to being able to get by more generally.

A third dynamic is the charitable response to food insecurity. Food banks (food pantries), soup kitchens, free budgeting advice, and cooking classes sprang up across rich liberal democracies as food insecurity began to emerge as a social problem. As social safety nets were unravelled and the welfare state receded in the 1980s, concerned citizens moved into the gap, seeking to ease the suffering of their neighbors. Beginning as temporary solutions to emerging hardship, food banks (food pantries) have become an embedded part of the systems which support the welfare of the most vulnerable people in rich liberal democracies. They simultaneously provide: well-intentioned charitable relief of hardship; an inadequate attempt to meet the needs of those suffering food insecurity; and a symbolic relief by non-governmental organizations of the state's responsibilities to care for its citizens.

Describing these dynamics clarifies some elements of the context in which food insecurity is persistently generated in rich liberal democracies. This social problem has its roots in the overarching structures of political economy, but is complicated by the dynamics of household structure, and of community structures. These dynamics also present the two sides of vulnerability—the negative impacts on people of the systems and structures in which they live, and the ability that people have to respond to, cope with, and recover from those effects. To reduce the incidence and negative outcomes of food insecurity in rich liberal democracies, policies must work either to reduce the negative impacts of systems, or to support people in their ability to cope with and recover from negative impacts.

The policy measures we describe below are internationally relevant, focussed on reducing the vulnerability to food insecurity in rich liberal democracies; some have been implemented to an extent in some of these countries. Importantly, household incomes are insufficient to ensure food security *in context*—the context being costs of living compared to income. We begin by addressing the income side of this equation with policies that adjust the situations that systems and structures are putting people in.

Avoiding vulnerability through employment

Ensuring the ability of workers to earn enough to support their household through paid employment will reduce vulnerability to food insecurity and so its incidence. There are any number of policies which might support income levels which reduce vulnerability, so here we focus on areas which have been highlighted in research concerning food insecurity. These policies seek to re-shape rather than radically re-structure the present political economies of rich liberal democracies. That is, these are policy solutions that fit within a modern capitalist system of political economy.

- **The payment of a living wage**—literally an income upon which people are able to live at a standard recognized as acceptable in rich liberal democracies. Where the lowest incomes are below the living wage, low-income households are more vulnerable to food insecurity. This measure also meets complaints about transfers of money by state welfare systems being so generous as to discourage people from earning money by working, as the payment of a living wage erases this "lack of incentive" to enter paid work.
- **Close the gender pay gap**. Women, and sole-parent households headed by a female, are more likely to suffer food insecurity. The gender dynamics *within* households increase the complexity of the gender-food insecurity relationship, but this aside, households relying on (lower on average) female incomes must attempt to meet the costs of living with less income. One option is to support the widespread practice of benchmarking jobs based on the skills, knowledge, responsibility, effort, and working conditions involved,

which offers the opportunity to erode gendered influences on employment income in a methodical way.

- **Provide a basic level of affordable and quality childcare.** Sole-parent households are more likely to suffer food insecurity. They live off one income and sole parents have half the time resources of a two-parent household to split between paid employment, childcare, unpaid housework and other commitments. Cheap childcare supports people entering and maintaining paid employment, and reduces the penalty of being raised by a time-poor caregiver-earner.

Avoiding vulnerability through adequate support

- A social safety net providing *cash transfers adequate to meet the costs of living*. Across rich liberal democracies, these transfers have become less and less adequate to meet the costs of living since the 1980s, as neoliberal rationality has influenced policy formation, often joining with the punitive moral positions of neoconservative ideology.
- A social safety net which provides *affordable social housing*. Housing is a major and inelastic cost of living in rich liberal democracies, so ensuring that this inelastic cost does not impinge on a household's ability to access food reduces its vulnerability to food insecurity. Social housing charged at a fixed percentage of weekly/monthly income, say 20–30%, is a practical
- A social safety net operating to *provide citizens with the support they are entitled to*. A significant barrier for people accessing support is bureaucratic prevarication at the point of access, and more recently, sanctions (withholding payments) imposed for infringement of rules or timeframes.
- A social safety net which *supports the ability of people to find and maintain employment*. Free or low-cost education and skills training with a view beyond immediate labor market shortages, to allow people to contribute to society as they are best able to. Other measures such as affordable public transport and childcare can also support this policy goal.

Avoiding vulnerability through capacity to cope

The other side of vulnerability from the outcomes of the systems that people live in is people being unable to manage or cope with the stresses they experience in those systems. Measures that address this side of vulnerability substantially involve actions which operate beyond or outside of market systems.

Policy which targets the education or training of people suffering food insecurity with cooking or gardening skills may have some limited positive impact—but it should not be considered as a viable means to broadly reduce vulnerability to food insecurity. If accessing food is a problem, cooking skills have little to be applied to, while access to a garden is interrupted by movement between rental properties, if one is available at all in urban settings; and in any case home gardens tend to provide access to the cheapest produce—that which is in season. It is true that some people could benefit from free garden or cooking training, and making this available would be a positive policy action, but making it compulsory for receivers of charitable or state assistance is unlikely to drive a significant reduction in vulnerability to food insecurity. However, the notion that looking to the past to improve relationships with food as a measure against food insecurity has significant potential—like supporting local food sovereignty. A relationship with food which usefully supports the reduction of vulnerability to food insecurity may well involve less distance, processing, middle-men, and ignorance.

- **Universal free and nutritious school lunches**. This measure is supported by evidence from some countries that this reduces the incidence and negative outcomes of food insecurity. The availability of a meal at school is not affected by household situations, so the provision of this food mitigates through stability the potential impact of household difficulties in accessing food security. This policy certainly has its critics: this meal is only available on school days, so that households face the cost of lunches at weekends and during school holidays, and this may cause difficulty in adjusting budgeting. However, this direct approach to ensuring (limited) access to food through the infrastructure of the public education system ensures consistency and certainty of food provision during term-time.
- **Policy support for (local) food sovereignty initiatives**. From community gardens to permaculture orchards on road verges and in parks, these initiatives have the potential to make whole communities less vulnerable to food insecurity, providing a reliable supplementary source of nutritious foods. Permaculture fruit trees and vines or nut trees can replace the ornamental greenery planted by local authorities in their cities and towns. Grassed land can be set aside for community gardens, with basic support like a shed or tools provided to kick-start moves towards community food sovereignty.

This set of policy measures address vulnerability to food insecurity by looking beyond market mechanisms.

These policy measures form a vulnerability-minimization approach to reducing the incidence of food insecurity in rich liberal democracies. They are intended to move the food-access situation for a significant minority of households away from "want despite plenty" and towards "provision from plenty." The pursuit of policy solutions to food insecurity must contend with neoliberal rationality and its rhetoric, push-back from groups who prefer the status-quo, and the situational complexities in which food insecurity is generated. The research evidence available supports action to bring change to the present situation. The possibilities for effective policy interventions exits. The benefits offer opportunities for many people, but especially for those members of social groups who disproportionately suffer food insecurity in rich liberal democracies.

Key Sources

Allen, P. (1999) Reweaving the Food Security Safety Net: Mediating Entitlement and Entrepreneurship, *Agriculture and Human Values*, 16(2): 117-129, DOI: 10.1023/a:1007593210496

Allen, P. (2007) The Disappearance of Hunger in America, *Gastronomica: The Journal of Food and Culture*, 7(3): 19-23, DOI: 10.1525/gfc.2007.7.3.19

Cohen, N., Poppendieck, J. and Freundenberg, N. (2017) Food Justice in the Trump Age: Priorities for Urban Food Adovcates, *Journal of Food Law & Policy*, 13: 43.

Coleman-Jensen, A., Rabbitt, M.P., Gregory, C.A. and Singh, A. (2017) Household Food Security in the United States in 2016, Retrieved from: https://www.ers.usda.gov/webdocs/publications/84973/err-237.pdf?v=42979

Cooper, N., Purcell, S. and Jackson, R. (2014) Below the Breadline: The Relentless Rise of Food Poverty in Britain, Retrieved from: https://www.trusselltrust.org/wp-content/uploads/sites/2/2016/01/Below-the-Breadline-The-Trussell-Trust.pdf

Dowler, E. and Finer, C.J. (2003) *Welfare of Food: Rights and Responsibilities in a Changing World*, Wiley-Blackwell.

Food Research and Action Centre (2015) *A Plan of Action to End Hunger in America*, Retrieved from: http://www.frac.org/wp-content/uploads/2016/10/plan-to-end-hunger-in-america.pdf

Kneafsey, M., Dowler, E., Lambie-Mumford, H., Inman, A. and Collier, R. (2013) Consumers and Food Security: Uncertain or Empowered?, *Journal of Rural Studies*, 29(0): 101-112, DOI: 10.1016/j.jrurstud.2012.05.005

Lambie-Mumford, H., Crossley, D., Jensen, E., Verbeke, M. and Dowler, E. (2014) *Household Food Security in the UK: A Review of Food Aid*, Retrieved from: https://www.gov.uk/government/uploads/system/uploads/attachment_data/file/283071/household-food-security-uk-140219.pdf

Poppendieck, J. (1998) *Sweet Charity?: Emergency Food and the End of Entitlement*, New York: Viking Penguin.

Riches, G. and Silvasti, T (eds) (2014) *First World Hunger Revisited: Food Charity or the Right to Food?*, Basingstoke: Palgrame Macmillan.

Shepherd, B. (2012) Thinking Critically about Food Security, *Security Dialogue*, 43(3): 195-212, D OI: 10.1177/0967010612443724

Tarasuk, V., Dachner, N. and Loopstra, R. (2014) Food Banks, Welfare, and Food Insecurity in Canada, *British Food Journal*, 116(9): 1405-1417, DOI: 10.1108/BFJ-02-2014-0077

Extending Old-Age Pension Coverage to Workers in the Informal Sector Economy in Ethiopia

Ajanaw Alemie, University of Gondar, Ethiopia and James L. Scherrer, Dominican University, USA

The Problem

S ocial security is a fundamental human right as well as a social and economic necessity as established in Article 25 of the United Nations Universal Declaration of Human Rights 1948. Governments increasingly recognize the economic stabilization social security provides, particularly in times of crisis. Because social security alleviates poverty and reduces inequality through income transfers, promotion of social justice, and economic growth, it is one of the conditions for sustainable economic and social development.

Old-age pension is one of the types of social security benefits. Although there has been much improvement in nations providing social security to the elderly, only 67.8% of the world population elderly receive formal social security benefits. Developing countries in particular have the challenging task of extending coverage to the poor and those working in the informal economy. In Africa, where only 29.6% of older persons have access to social security, this presents one of the biggest barriers that must be addressed to achieve significant poverty alleviation (International Labor Organization, 2017).

The United Nations has recognized the significant increase in the aging population worldwide. In sub-Saharan Africa, not only is there an increase in elderly persons, but also poverty among them is more pronounced, because formal social protection plans fail to reach large segments of the population, who work in the informal economy, while existing informal support systems are being undermined by rapid economic social and demographic changes. . The informal economy is comprised of very small, unregistered companies, household-based production, or agricultural production. Workers in the informal economy are often low-paid, or self-employed, or migrant. (Ginneken, 2003) Between 80 and 90% of the elderly have worked exclusively in the informal economy and are no longer able to engage in full-time work

Sustainable and inclusive growth, poverty alleviation, and inequality reduction require nations to provide a social safety net for their citizens. Such safety nets prevent poverty recidivism due to income reductions from social risks, such as sickness, employment injury, and old age. Naturally, this safety net would include social security solutions for workers in the informal economy. Nations have begun to recognize the social justice importance of providing social protection to informal workers.

Social pension plans play an important role in reducing elderly poverty and vulnerability, help to break the intergenerational poverty cycle, and bring economic, social and health benefits to the elderly recipients and their families. Social security for the elderly is a right that the aged have that is clearly embodied in human rights instruments and international labor standards. As a result, a universal old-age pension plan will provide the best means of alleviating poverty among all older people as well as improving their wellbeing, nutrition and health.

Most pension systems provide at least basic protection against the risks associated with old age for formal sector workers, but exclude those who have worked in the informal sector. Old-age pension coverage rates are low in many developing countries not only due to high rates of employment informality, but also a lack of legal or administrative infrastructures necessary to cover informal workers. This, failure to participate in a pension system when combined with the weakening of family support networks due to urbanization, migration, industrialization, and HIV/AIDS contributes significantly to the increase in poverty among elderly retirees from the informal economy.

Research Evidence

The informal economy is growing worldwide. Informal workers and their enterprises are a permanent feature of both urban and rural life. In developing countries, most jobs are generated in the informal sector, where more than 80% of all workers are employed. This significant growth in the informal sector economy is due to the persistence of poverty and the increasing number of people who do not have access to social security (Francie, 2009). The informal economy is used as a coping mechanism for families and individuals whose earning opportunities are limited. The informal economy is also used to escape state regulations, perceived to be onerous, such as income taxes.

One of the key global problems facing social security today is the fact that more than half of the world's populations are excluded from any type of formal social security protection. They tend to be part of the informal economy, and are outside the scope of contribution-based social insurance plans. The limited coverage of the formal social security system creates serious challenges for providing adequate income security to the elderly. This issue is more severe in developing countries partly due to logistical, economic and educational difficulties in getting informal sector workers to participate in pension plans.

An example of the problem of providing social security to the elderly who have been workers in the informal economy, that applies to all of Africa is Ethiopia where older people make up between 3.5 and 5% of the population, comprising between 2.98 and 4.26 million people. Most of these have no form of secure income. What income they do have is provided through their families, community transfers, or money earned from their part-time labor. Only 1.4% of the retired elderly have any regular public-sector pension. The remainder of the elderly population rely on their families and their communities for support.

Ninety percent of the employed population in Ethiopia work for either the informal sector, the private sector, or are self-employed. Formal social security measures are largely unavailable to this population. Consequently, they have a heightened vulnerability to income instability and poverty, especially in their old age (Emerta, 2010). In reality, most of the older people in the country, who account for 4.3% of the total population, live in destitution, often falling in the category of "chronically poor" and unable to afford basic services. Social protection plans, such as the productive safety net program, have aggravated their condition because most older people are labor constrained or without productive assets.

Ethiopia, like many other developing countries in Africa, has inadequately developed safety nets, pension systems and public transfers. Because of this inadequacy, the population, particularly the elderly, have to rely on traditional systems including family and community transfers. These systems, however, are faced with economic and social shocks. HIV/AIDS, and other health problems that have significantly reduced their efficacy. Social justice principles require the nation to take more responsibility in providing social security services as a poverty alleviation measure.

For many people across Africa, aging is accompanied by chronic and deepening poverty. Migration, conflict, natural disasters and the impact of HIV/AIDS has weakened family and community supports upon which they have relied. Currently, less than 10% of Africa's workforce are covered by social security programs (Bailey and Turner, 2002). Therefore, informal sector workers and those working in subsistence farming continue to be socio-economically excluded, increasing their chances of living in poverty. The major challenge facing social security programs in Africa is to scale-up their coverage to address this growing problem. Countries in Africa are also confronted with the challenge of strengthening familial and informal social protection systems. Among the best practices identified in Africa in dealing with the challenge of aging, are the Republic of South Africa, Mauritius and Tunisia. The Republic of South Africa has a commendable old-age grant provided monthly to its elderly citizens who are without other means of regular income support. Other countries with similar grants are Botswana, Lesotho, Mauritius, and Namibia. In all these countries the grants were found to substantially reduce poverty rates among older persons.

Recommendations and Solutions

Introducing Universal Old-Age Pension to Workers in the Informal Sector

The formal social security system in Ethiopia dates to the formation of the Pension and Social Security Authority (PSSA) in 1963. Currently, the PSSA administers four pension plans, namely: old-age pension, invalidity pension, sickness benefits, and work injury pension (Emerta, 2010). Recently, Ethiopia has enacted new pension laws that would give benefits to the permanent workers of private organizations. This recent activity, while welcome, fails to address the social security assistance needs of all the poor, elderly people who have worked in and retired from the informal sector. As compared to some African countries pension plans, it is not comprehensive in its nature. To mention some, Botswana and Mauritius have universal old-age pension, Lesotho (non-contributory old-age pension plan), South Africa (means-tested old-age pension), Liberia and Namibia (old-age pension) (Bailey and Turner, 2002). The PSSA should develop a pension plan for this group that will effectively reduce old-age dependence, poverty, and vulnerability, and promote social justice. Universal social pensions are financially sustainable and attract a large measure of political support. It is estimated that a 100 Birr pension for all Ethiopians over the age of 65 would cost around 1% of the GDP, an affordable cost.

The means-tested approach undermines citizenship principles and the rights-based approach to social security. Eligibility can be contested. Administrative costs require more resources and capacity than the universal approach. Faulty targeting can leave many elders impoverished. Adverse incentive effects and possible induced changes in household types in order to claim a pension are additional concerns. While means-tested social pensions are fiscally sustainable even in developing countries, their operational feasibility is considered to be weak.

In contrast, universal social pensions are administratively feasible. They enhance equity and inclusion, by avoiding the discrimination and corruption that can occur where means-tests are applied, as well as build social solidarity, and are often politically more acceptable. Because they cost less than 2% of the Gross Domestic Product (GDP), universal social pensions are affordable even in very poor countries. The universal version of the social pension is superior to the means-tested version in developing countries, particularly for rural communities. Since aging households experience greater exclusion from market-based protection as well as from informal (household-based) protection, universal social pension program coverage would be much more effective and inclusive in its operation. Universal social pensions have economic, social, and health benefits. They have been found to significantly reduce levels of old-age poverty, as well as improve the wellbeing, nutrition, and health of the elderly. Moreover, universal pensions have been found to be an important policy tool for wider development objectives. They have been found to improve the wellbeing of children in the context of HIV/AIDS and high levels of migration, which have left older people as main caregivers for orphans and grandchildren. They have also been shown to contribute to economic development in a range of ways, through boosting investment and stimulating consumption.

Universal social pensions may have some potential limitations. The concerns include the fear that such expenditures would divert scarce resources from "productive sectors," as well as apprehensions that such policies would create dependency. They may also discourage participation in contributory social security plans and cause families and communities to feel less responsible for the economic security of their elders. National administrative capacity to effectively implement these programs with adequate financial controls would be an ongoing concern. Finally, elders with access to social pensions may become vulnerable to financial or other abuse. Despite these potential challenges, the introduction of universal social pensions could be feasible and successful if it is based on strong political commitment, administrative capacity, and community and stakeholders participation.

Strengthening Community-Based Social Protection Plans

Community-based social protection (CBSP) plans can be effective in reaching the elderly poor, particularly when used in conjunction with a universal pension system. CBSPs are most effective on a small scale and can ensure that targeting those who qualify is effectively accomplished by the pension system. They can supplement the pension system when it does not adequately meet the needs of the elderly participants. In those instances where universal pensions are differentially distributed, they can ensure that such distribution is fair and according to the needs of the recipients. Thus, a collaborative effort between CBSPs and national governments can ensure that poverty alleviation and the wellbeing of the elderly are ensured.

Creating a Network of Collaboration Among Various Stakeholders

Stakeholders include a broad range of groups and organizations that often work at cross purposes to each other and to CBSPs. This can lead to competition and chaos in ensuring that the elderly receive the support they need. Governments are in an excellent position to bring these stakeholders together to work collaboratively in addressing the social needs of the elderly. Universal social pension programs can be used to encourage these groups to work together to ensure that the relevant funds reach their intended recipients. These stakeholders include international organizations such as the United Nations (and its various agencies), and the World Bank. National, regional, and local governments can also be brought into this collaborative effort. Finally social security institutions, employers, workers' unions, non-governmental organizations and community-based organizations can be engaged in significant and cooperative ways. In implementing the policy, the presence of trained social workers at each level of government administration will be needed to manage the universal pension programs and ensure social justice as well as collaboration between all stakeholders.

Lobbying and Policy Advocacy

The drivers of change encompasses both formal and non-formal groups and organizations, including NGOs, political groups and parties, national and international organizations, and other groups and individuals that can assert pressure upon the political system to encourage the introduction of universal social pension to workers in the informal sector in Ethiopia. Such policy and advocacy groups can boost the will of the nation to move forward in providing a universal pension for its elderly. It can bring people together to ensure that policy makers consider the needs of this group and ensure that a fair and socially just system is developed. They can also monitor the implementation of the program to identify where faults may occur or inefficiencies are developed. They can thus protect the elderly from fraud or other criminal activity that preys on the vulnerabilities of the aged population.

While these solutions are provided for the Ethiopian context, they are readily adaptable to similar issues that have not been adequately addressed in other African nations in their own contexts. The concept of universal old-age pension for elderly workers in the informal sector can be applied in other nations in ways that are affordable. Strengthening community-based social protection plans and creating networks of collaboration between stakeholders take advantage of already existing structures and strengthen them. Finally, policy advocacy can bring the plight of the elderly informal workers to the attention of policy makers while providing a way to address them.

References

Agravat, D.R. and Kaplelach, S. (2017) Effect of demographic characteristics on micro-pension uptake among informal employees of Kenya Ports Authority, *Journal of Business and Strategic Management*, 2(2): 95-117.

Anders, M. (2017) Can a new pension plan offer security to informal workers in Ghana?, Accessed at https://www.devex.com/news/can-a-new-pension-plan-offer-security-to-informal-workers-in-Ghana-91296 on December 31, 2017.

African Union (2011) Social protection plan for the informal economy and rural workers 2011–2015, *8th Ordinary Session of the Labour and Social Affairs Commission of the African Union* April 11–15, 2011. Yaounde, Cameroon.

Bailey, C. and Turner, J. (2002) Social security in Africa, *Journal of Aging and Social Policy*, (14)1: 105-114, DOI 10.1300/J031v14n01_09.

Browne. E. (2013) *Community-based social protection (GSDRC Helpdesk Research Report 1020)*, Birmingham, UK: GSDRC, University of Birmingham.

Emerta, A. (2010) Adopting private pension system in Ethiopia, *The African Symbosium: An online journal of African educational research network*, 10 (1): 7–13.

Ginneken, W. (2003) *Extending Social Security Policies for Developing Countries*, ESS Working Paper No. 13. Social Security Policy and Development Branch, ILO Office.

Hu, Y. and Stewart, F. (2009) Pension coverage and informal sector workers: international experience, *OECD Working Paper on Insurance and Private Pensions No. 31* OECD Publishing. DOI: 10.1787/227432837078.

International Labour Organization (2017) *World social protection report: Universal social protection to achieve the Sustainable Development Goals 2017–2019*, Geneva: International Labour Office.

Jessica, K. and Johnson, M. (2008) An assessment of the importance and feasibility of universal non-contributory pension plans for low–income countries, *International Studies on Social Security, Volume 13*, Belgium: Intersentia. Graduate School of Social Work and Chestnut Hill, MA: Boston College.

Lwanga-Ntale, C., Rusinow, A. and Knox, C. (2011) Social protection for older people in the context of economic growth: the case for Ethiopia-issues, opportunities and choices, in *Proceedings of the Seventh Annual Conference of the Ethiopian Society of Sociologists, Social Workers and Anthropologists (ESSWA)*, Addis Ababa, Ethiopia.

United Nations (1949) United Nations Universal Declaration of Human Rights, New York: United Nations.

SIXTEEN

Tackling Digital Exclusion: Counter Social Inequalities Through Digital Inclusion

Massimo Ragnedda

The Problem

Information and Communication Technologies (ICTs) have granted many privileges to their users. At the same time, they have given rise to new and complex forms of exclusion affecting those already marginalized and disempowered. The development of the information society has highlighted the existence of obstacles preventing certain social groups from accessing and properly using technologies. This limited access and use of ICTs is defined as the "digital divide."

Those who are digitally included can more easily access services that impact positively on their health, occupation, education, and housing. Therefore, an exclusion from, or even partial access to, the digital realm has become a significant source of social inequality. However, accessing the internet, alone, is simply not enough to be digitally included. Indeed, it is also necessary to have the capacity to use, create, successfully navigate, and understand online content. These are the skills necessary to be a digitally literate individual once the technology is available. Digital literacy, therefore, indicates the ability to utilize digital infrastructure and not simply to access it. Digital inclusion, then, refers to the policies that will bridge the digital divide and support digital literacy. It tackles social inequalities by providing solutions for socially disadvantaged citizens to easily access and effectively use ICTs to improve their quality of life.

This chapter will explain strategies that public, private, and voluntary sectors should follow to reduce digital exclusion and promote digital and social equity. These strategies are intended to ensure that people who are disadvantaged in terms of age, gender, ethnicity, location (urban or rural), or disability can access and enjoy the benefits of the information society. Digital inclusion initiatives are designed to give citizens the right access, skills, trust, and motivation to confidently go online. Digital inclusion projects aim to enhance the capacity to use ICTs in ways that promote engagement and well-being and, therefore, to counter social inequalities.

Research Evidence

Recent studies of the digital divide show how insufficient and unequal access to the internet can create new forms of social segregation that exacerbate already existing social inequalities. Digital exclusion can lead to social exclusion affecting negative life outcomes related to health, income, and education, among others. Access to, and use of, ICTs should be considered as a new civil right—an essential necessity to be a full citizen in the networked society. In a digital-reliant society, where the internet is diffused into all sectors of society, being excluded from the digital realm means missing opportunities to improve one's quality of life. Those at the margin of the digital world are being left behind, further reinforcing inequalities they are already suffering in society.

However, it would be wrong to assume that individuals' access to the internet can be automatically transformed into other social outcomes. Indeed, the digital divide should not be seen as a simple matter of access, nor approached as solely a technological problem. In the early years of the spread of computers and the internet, the digital divide was perceived as a one-dimensional gap between social classes' differential possession of technologies. Policy makers thought that the only way to bridge the digital divide was to reduce the gap between those who connect and those who do not by offering cheaper and faster physical access. However, enhancing the access alone (reducing the first level of the digital divide) does not close the gap of multidimensional digital inequalities, which reinforce existing social inequalities and create new forms of exclusion from the job market, governmental institutions, leisure, and educational activities.

To tackle digital inequalities and promote a more inclusive society, it is not enough to offer low-cost and more reliable Internet access, since this is only one of the elements involved in the digital inclusion process. Mark Warschauer, in his book *Technology and Social Inclusion*, explains four types of digital resources necessary for effective inclusion:

1. physical (possession of computer and connectivity);
2. human (education and ICT literacy);

3. digital (relevant content in one's language);
4. social (institutional and society structures supporting access and use).

The digital divide tends to change as technology progresses, so policy makers need to adapt and update their strategies to suit new contexts. To gain the full advantages of the opportunities offered by ICTs, social science research suggest that the following individual factors need to be considered with Internet usage, digital skills; motivations, autonomy, self-confidence; and attitudes. These factors make a qualitatively different digital experience between users, impacting the length and extent of internet use, which are the base of the second-level digital divide. These further elements give a better idea of the multidimensionality of the digital inclusion process that cannot be approached as a matter of basic access alone. Therefore, to address digital inclusion, policy makers need to also provide digital skills and digital literacy training, which have been shown to yield positive effects on social inclusion and rates of political participation, positively effecting the democratic process.

In a digital-reliant society it is vital that everyone has the digital skills they need to fully participate in society. It is crucial that effective digital skills and digital literacy programmes will ensure that the workforce is prepared for future technological changes. The benefits of digital inclusion projects go well beyond the single citizen and affect the community as a whole. Thus, to build a digitally inclusive society, we need to involve all sectors of society, to ensure that all citizens are able to access, use, and understand the benefits of ICTs. Full digital inclusion requires that we provide all citizens with affordable access to ICTs, and eliminate social, knowledge-based, and physical accessibility barriers. It is more urgent than ever to ensure universal access and digital literacy. A digital-ready citizen is not only able to navigate the web, but they are also able to manage their online identity and appropriately handle all personal and sensitive information online. Digital literacy initiatives can provide social and mental health benefits by helping individuals stay in touch with relatives and friends using ICTs, thus reducing feelings of loneliness. These types of tangible outcomes deriving from effective use of ICTs are at the base of what I call the third level of the digital divide. Any attempt to tackle social inequalities with ICTs, needs to take into consideration three levels of the digital divide: 1) inequalities in access; 2) differences in usage skills; and 3) tangible outcomes of internet use. A digital inclusion strategy will have positive impacts on social inclusion only by giving everybody the possibility to access, effectively use, and gain advantages from ICTs.

Recommendations and Solutions

The best social policy promotes digital inclusion to make the benefits of ICTs and internet usage available to all citizens, and particularly to open the door to the socially disadvantaged at the margins of social and digital realms. Successful digital inclusion projects not merely offer the possibility to access digital content, but also offer the necessary support to acquire the knowledge for proper and independent use of those technologies. Furthermore, effective digital inclusion initiatives train low-literacy citizens and prepare them for jobs in information-focused industries, where a high level of digital skills is required. On a broader term, digital inclusion initiatives not simply support well informed global citizens, but also nurture digital citizens that are socially integrated in order to pursue fulfilling lives.

The best digital inclusion programs are designed to enhance civic engagement, allowing full participation in community affairs and connections with local and national agencies for all citizens, regardless of social background. Best practice social policies are offered by communities providing digital inclusion projects that involve everyone in decision-making processes that affect citizens' online and offline worlds. Best practices also involve giving citizens access to free services provided by local and national governments, as well as teaching them the digital skills they need to help them live better lives. Ultimately, digital divide policies and practices will enhance the quality of life of citizens who can access and efficiently use ICTs for community participation and engagement to fulfill their human needs and creative interests.

If barriers to digital inclusion are not addressed, there is a danger that the digital divide will further increase inequality by cementing existing social divides. For this reason, it is also important to understand the reasons for non-use, to develop strategies for digitally including those at the margins of the digital world, and to demonstrate the significance and importance that digital technologies can have upon their lives. These understandings are vital in order to create a better and more inclusive society.

Policy makers and communities, throughout their institutions, processes, and public awareness efforts, can concretely help communities to be digitally inclusive in three different ways, respectively related with the aforementioned three levels of the digital divide.

1. *Provide free or affordable access to ICTs.*

Accessing the internet means not only accessing digital content, but also accessing services, resources, and opportunities. However, not everybody can access digital content. To address this problem, governments may need to implement new policies and infrastructure, to digitally include citizens by giving them the possibilities to access the internet, providing free access to digital technologies, including hardware, software, and high-speed internet. This could be done in several ways, such as offering public access computers, offering free wifi hotspots, or partnering with broadband providers to offer low-cost broadband or low-cost options for home computer purchasing. Moreover, access to ICTs for people with disabilities, with their full participation to the digital realm, should be guaranteed. These initiatives offer a wide range of otherwise excluded content to their users, particularly to those marginalized and vulnerable people and households that cannot afford the devices, services, and connection speeds required to fully access and use the internet. Bridging the first level of digital divide by offering to everyone the possibility to access the internet through an affordable and reliable service, including high-speed connectivity, is the first step in reducing digital inequalities in today's digital society.

2. *Have community institutions provide digital literacy projects (libraries, schools, etc.) to meet diverse local needs.*

As we have seen, access alone is not enough to counteract digital inequalities and tackle social and digital exclusion. Digital inclusion initiatives must also meet citizens' needs, by providing skills and literacy training to help individuals develop the abilities to confidently use computers and the internet to solve everyday problems met in the digital environment. Assisting citizens in using ICTs, in navigating the web, and in evaluating and creating digital content, is vital to tackle the second level of digital divide. By providing knowledge and digital resources, individuals might enjoy the use of ICTs and make it a satisfactory experience and, therefore, lead to a more equal society and greater economic opportunities. Digital literacy and digital skills training need to be delivered in trusted and comfortable locations (libraries, recreation centres, schools, etc.) and supported by trained instructors. It is necessary to provide content, services and resources tailored upon citizen's interests. For instance, senior digital literacy projects may focus on the basic digital training, while youth digital skills initiatives might guide young people toward professional technology use and enhance civic participation, while other digital training projects may offer guidance and support for small businesses interested in widening their horizon and move into the digital market.

3.   Provide ICT content and services tied to tangible social service outcomes
Finally, digital literacy and digital skills projects can help in reducing the third level of the digital divide by providing assistance and services in using ICTs to get some tangible results, thus reducing inequalities in the concrete outcomes deriving from the use of the internet. More specifically, successful digital inclusion strategies help citizens on a wide array of fields, such as job seeking, information retrieval, sociability, savings, employment, familial relationships, and offering improved learning opportunities. In this way, social institutions and policy makers are helping citizens to use ICTs to enhance their career, education or social and cultural life, and, at the same time, improving the whole community in which they are involved. Effective digital inclusion may positively affect community health care needs by providing more services and resources to those who need them the most. This is particularly true for the most disadvantaged and underserved social groups that, through the use of ICTs, can access services and support that they otherwise would not. Digital literacy projects need to focus on the outcome, rather than on the technology, training citizens how to take advantage of the economic, educational, and social opportunities available through ICTs.

Tackling digital inequalities is a way to reduce social inequalities. The role of policy makers in driving digital inclusion is increasingly important, since citizens need not only access to the digital world (shrinking the first level of digital divide), but also the right skills, motivation and trust (second level of digital divide) to understand and enjoy the benefits of digital inclusion and get some tangible outcomes from it (third level of digital divide). This is particularly true for the most socially disadvantaged people (in regard to social class, age, race/ ethnicity, physical ability, etc.), which more than others, tend to rely on public institutions as the means of accessing the digital realm and all the services which are increasingly moving online. All citizens need to have the relevant access, confidence, literacy, motivation, and skills to properly access and navigate the web. An exclusion from this world full of opportunities and resources may further exacerbate deep-rooted inequalities.

Public institutions are becoming the frontline for a variety of government and local authority services, providing access and support for those who wish to access and use the internet. These institutions, when well equipped and supported by local or national governments, are crucial to serving the public in digital-literacy and digital-inclusion capacities. Policy makers need to make sure that citizens understand the full benefits deriving from an appropriate and effective way to use ICTs and how these uses may contribute to improve their quality of life and create an engaged community.

Key Resources

Bertot, J.C, Jaeger, P.T. and McClure, C.R. (eds) (2011) *Public Libraries and the Internet: Roles, Perspectives, and Implications*, Westport, CT: Libraries Unlimited.

Thompson, K.M., Jaeger, P.T., Greene Taylor, N., Subramaniam, M. and Bertot, J.C. (2014) *Digital Literacy and Digital Inclusion: Information Policy and the Public Library*, Lanham, MD: Rowman & Littlefield.

Ragnedda, M. (2017) *The Third Digital Divide: A Weberian Approach to Digital Inequalities,* Abingdon, UK: Routledge.

Ragnedda, M. and Muschert, G.W. (eds) (2013) *The Digital Divide: The Internet and Social Inequality in International Perspective*, Abingdon, UK: Routledge.

Ragnedda, M. and Muschert, G.W. (eds) (2017) *Theorizing Digital Divides*, Abingdon, UK: Routledge.

Real, B., McDermott, A.J., Bertot, J.C. and Jaeger, P.T. (2015) Digital Inclusion and the Affordable Care Act: Public Libraries, Politics, Policy, and Enrolment in 'Obamacare', *Public Library Quarterly*, 34(1): 1-22.

Selwyn, N. (2003) Apart from Technology: Understanding People's Non-use of Information and Communication Technologies in Everyday Life, *Technology in Society*, 25(1): 99-116.

Selwyn, N. and Gorard, S. (2004) Exploring the Role of ICT in Facilitating Adult Informal Learning Education, *Communication and Information*, 4(2): 293-310.

Van Dijk, J.A.G.M. (2005) *The Deepening Divide: Inequality in the Information Society*, London: Sage.

Warschauer, M. (2003) *Technology and Social Inclusion: Rethinking the Digital Divide*, London: The MIT Press.

SECTION VI

Looking Forward

SEVENTEEN

Global Issues

Jon Shefner and Michelle Christian

T he pace of economic globalization has increased since 1990, according to most sources. Although this increased integration of economies is celebrated by many, this volume suggests many reasons for concern. As the volume authors demonstrate, a number of problems are clearly linked to neoliberal globalization. The simultaneous prioritization of market logic and attack on state resolution of social needs are key similarities across the volume. One of the contributions of this volume is the diagnosis of shared globalization-driven problems, but the volume is further distinguished by the fact that authors' diagnoses are matched in each case by potential policy solutions. Here, we similarly diagnose general trends in labor, environment, and global governance, and offer some general solutions as a way to help contextualize the authors' more precise contributions.

Labor

In the neoliberal era, workers bear the brunt of increasingly polarized global inequality in wealth and income. The world of work continues to be marred by global, national, and local stratification forces that determine who gets good jobs or bad jobs, what those workers look like, and where they come from. According to the International Labour Organization (ILO), 1.4 billion people, 42% of the world's total employment population in 2017, struggle with "vulnerable employment." Vulnerable employment, alternatively called precarious work, represents work that is informal, part-time, irregular, low-pay, lacking security and benefits, and disposable. Ninety percent of workers in India fall into this category, as does much of sub-Saharan Africa, where people toil between subsistence farming to self-employed work informality. In the Global North, work precarity is seen in the rise of part-time contract work and service-based employment. Labor intermediaries, such as temporary staffing agencies or labor brokers who recruit workers for agriculture or light manufacturing, have gained new prominence as employers prefer to outsource their employer responsibilities.

Precarity is also reflective of gender, race, caste, class, and citizenship divisions. Women continue to be numerous in occupations and sectors that are constructed as feminine and subsequently not accorded equitable compensation and treatment. Migrant workers, 150 million in 2017, are crossing the globe—pulled by political instability, poverty, and neoliberal policies—to work in jobs where their migrant status is exploited for employer economic gain. As migrant workers they embody a "precarity multiplier" that worsens all standard employment conditions. Internal migrant precarious worker status is just as jarring in many locales. The Chinese and Indian economies could not function without internal migrants. In China an estimated 260 million rural migrant workers, controlled by the state-run *hukou* system, which dictates mobility and social protection, populate cities where they work in export factories, build high-rise buildings, and occupy the myriad of service jobs that keep cities running. Technological shifts in automation also shape the nature of work and growth in precarity. Increased polarization of good and bad jobs in the Global North is expected to grow, as almost 50% of jobs are projected to be at risk from automation. Global South workplaces are also at risk of job displacement in varying degrees.

These trends make for a challenging labor rights advocacy environment. The growth of precarity in the United States notably follows the weakening of industrial unions. The situation of labor in the Global South is even more dire, where labor organizers remain at great danger from state-sanctioned employer and police crackdowns and acts of violence. In 2012, a Bangladeshi labor organizer with the Bangladesh Centre for Worker Solidarity was killed and others were arrested and tortured. In 2014, Cambodian garment workers were shot during a street protest for higher wages. Global corporations who outsource and offshore production to factories in these regions have done very little to mitigate these repressive acts. Despite this context, as we discuss below, promising new avenues for transnational worker organizing are also forming.

Policy Options

- **Innovative Organizing 1.** New innovative organizing techniques have formed over the last decade to counter the challenges found in contemporary global capitalism. Organizing traditionally marginalized workers, such as women and service workers, and organizing across the supply chain are two such tactics. First, the success of such organizing campaigns as the passage of ILO Convention 189 in 2013, the convention on domestic workers, showcases how a grassroots, cross-national, and ally-connected campaign led by women-of-color workers from the Global South can succeed. Domestic workers, once labeled "unorganizable," are leading the way in spotlighting how to collectively organize in the 21st century.

- **Innovative Organizing 2.** The complexity of today's global economy in which transnational corporations control fragmented and dispersed global supply chains has elicited a new form of organizing across the supply chain. Cutting-edge campaigns, such as those around Walmart's vast global supply chain, which target subcontractors and logistics workers, are showing how to build a worker solidarity movement across borders. Furthermore, such organizing also spotlights the emergence of a new, important corporate actor to organize around: the big supplier.

- **Innovative Organizing 2.** Globalization's spread of production means that any individual workplace stoppage is less disruptive than previous uses of strikes. This means that simultaneity of multiple workplace disruption has become more important. Although such strikes are difficult to organize, the same communication technologies that have have facilitated the expansion of the globalized economy can be used to harness it for workers' needs.

- **Basic Income Initiatives.** Pursuing wide-reaching basic income initiatives would mitigate the fallout from increased worker insecurity and the growth of precarious work, in addition to help offset ecological destruction caused by resource-depleting industries, as workers could shift their time to generative reproductive care. Proponents of basic income have been around for over a century, but the policy option has picked up prominence since the 2008 Great Recession and its massive inequality fallout. The Basic Income Earth Network has been a global advocate since 1986, counting members from all over the world including Brazil, Mexico, New Zealand, Slovenia, and the United States, to name just a few. The main principles of basic income, often called universal basic income, include the right of individuals in a community to have regular income that provides basic security around housing and food in an attempt to create what Guy Standing, in his 2017 book *Basic Income*, refers to as an "equality of basic living standards." Income would be paid to each person as an individual, regardless of marital or household status, and not require anything in return. Multiple locales throughout the globe have expressed interest in pursuing basic income initiatives. In 2016, Switzerland held a national referendum on basic income. Although the referendum failed, the movement behind it won global media attention. Also, in 2016, the government of Mexico City included a basic income provision in its new city constitution; and, in 2017 the state of Jammu and Kashmir in India announced their intention to phase in a basic income initiative.

Environment

Global environmental degradation has increased dramatically. Air pollution has worsened in many cities, deforestation is impacting whole continents, while water is polluted by both agricultural runoff and human waste. The human cost of ongoing environmental damage is dramatic: there are 1.8 million unsafe-water-related deaths in the Asian Pacific area alone, while unsafe water added to air pollution accounts for hundreds of thousands of premature deaths in West Asia and Africa.

Perhaps most notable, and linked to other environmental hazards, are the increases evident in the extent and rapidity of climate change. According to the Intergovernmental Panel on Climate Change, "Each of the last three decades has been successively warmer at the Earth's surface than any preceding decade since 1850. The period from 1983 to 2012 was likely the warmest 30-year period of the last 1400 years in the Northern Hemisphere." A warming climate is linked to greater frequency and severity of storms, both coastal and interior flooding, desertification, and more severe incidents of wildfire often linked to drought, currently and in the future. The average annual cost of climatic disasters has increased drastically.

When Global North readers envision these disasters and costs, events such as European flooding and California wildfires may be the most prominent in their minds. However, just as previous studies of environmental justice showed that disadvantaged populations were most likely to be subjected to national environmental harms such as toxic waste, poor nations in tropical areas are much more vulnerable to climatic disasters than their Northern counterparts. Within poor nations, the exposure to climate change is higher for those who are poorer, or work in certain jobs largely staffed by minorities and women. For many, their vulnerability is based on the fact that their livelihoods are directly sensitive to climate change: agricultural workers, forest dwellers, and those that make their living on the water are all likely to be some of the frontline victims of climate change. In addition to those workers are urban dwellers whose informal communities are often endangered by massive rain and mudslides.

Although global policy makers are taking important steps to address climate change and other global environmental hazards, efforts to remediate these hazards were partially stymied by the US Congress during the Obama era. To overcome Congressional intransigence, President Obama resorted to executive orders to impose healthier environmental standards and a regulatory process that prioritized reversing environmental degradation. Unfortunately, those executive orders have proven vulnerable to reversal under a Trump administration that is not only anti-science, but beholden to corporate interests whose profits conflict with sensible climate change policy. For example, Trump announced opening of more public lands and coasts to oil drilling while announcing tariffs on foreign-manufactured solar panels. These policies, coupled with the alleged desire to revive coal production, demonstrate a clear unwillingness to confront climate change. Despite the US status as the world's second-largest polluter, a variety of policies to reverse environmental degradation and climate change have been articulated. As the predominant economic power of the United States is increasingly balanced by other national or multinational powers, such as China, Russia, and the European Union, policy innovation and leadership is rapidly ceded to other global actors. The global agreement regarding the danger of climate change and environmental degradation has also led to powerful policy solutions from prestigious scientific voices such as the Intergovernmental Panel on Climate Change and the UN Environment Programme. Ongoing policy resolutions that address the damage posed by the twin dilemmas of climate change and structural inequalities include the following.

Policy Options

Recent analyses suggest an integrated approach to climate policy, one that integrates an understanding of structured inequalities and that brings all stakeholders into discussion (United Nations 2016).

Specific policies include the following.

- Diminish use of fossil fuels by stripping subsidies from companies that supply fossil fuels.

- Reward use of alternative fuel sources with the same kind of subsidies that large energy corporations have enjoyed for decades.
- Tax energy sources by the carbon content of the fuel.
- Increase research and development resources not only on alternative energy sources and energy storage, but also in remediation of local hazards suffered by vulnerable populations.
- Nurture attempts to reduce deforestation by paying poor nations and their residents not to cut forests, and to help find alternative work, including turning to the farming or production of biofuels.
- Increase access to clean technologies for poor nations.
- Increase food access to reduce "food miles," or the transport cost of shipping food.

Global Governance

The areas of workers' rights and environmental degradation, the issues we have raised, like those of all the authors in this volume, are centered around equity. In this section too, we focus on problems of equity among international governance institutions; some solutions to global governance inequity would also address other inequities we've pointed out. Those inequities are apparent in both policy and process of international institutions.

One of the clearest indications of inequity in policy is the effective paralysis in moving past the Doha round of negotiations held among members of the World Trade Organization.

The Doha, Qatar negotiations round that began in 2001 were meant to be the "development" round, addressing many of the objections poorer nations had to earlier WTO policy decisions. The key sticking point has been subsidies to Global North-based agricultural corporations, which not coincidentally often use petroleum based or other polluting chemicals. The search for an even playing field in this area would increase opportunities for Global South farmers to sell their products without being choked by the unfair advantages of transnational corporations with, not only vast economic power, but enormous resources for research and development subsidized by powerful nations. Importantly, poor and middle-income nations were not seeking to overthrow neoliberalism in these negotiations, but merely to have the same rules apply across the globe. The developing nations' desire to further open markets was fully consistent with neoliberalism.

Negotiations in Nairobi, Kenya in 2015 appeared to resolve some of these policy equity issues, especially regarding export subsidies, which were to be removed by 2018. The devil is always in the detail, however, as various exceptions were included which are likely to diminish the coverage of export subsidies. Additionally, it needs to be recognized that the line between export and domestic subsidies is not clear. Subsidies can be structured and packaged in various ways, so that an export subsidy can be replaced by the same subsidy provided as a domestic subsidy. Depending on the new form it takes, the change in a particular subsidy's impact on trade and equity might not be great. Indeed, the Nairobi package does not rein in domestic agriculture subsidies generally. These subsidies remain high and are proliferating. This is not just a rich-world problem any more; middle-income developing countries such as India are now big providers as well. In effect, the WTO has become the playground where nations tried to out-market each other. Both the dominance of large powers and the paralysis of any movement into fair trade are likely only to continue as the Trump administration brings protectionism back into trade negotiations, most recently manifested in both the imposition of large tariffs on foreign-made products such as washing machines and solar panels, as well as his expressed interest of making NAFTA "fairer" for the United States.

Inequity in policy mirrors inequity in process, most clearly demonstrated by the unequal levels of power in international bodies. The United Nations provides an immediate example: although majority rule allows greater voice for the predominantly poor and middle-income member nations, the ongoing dominance of a Security Council with permanent seats is held by the United States, the United Kingdom, France, China, and the Russian Federation. With these seats held by more powerful nations who have embraced neoliberal reforms to large extent, the possibility for true economic reform is limited. For example, the limited power and funding from member states of United Nation institutions, such as the UN Refugee Agency, have hampered its ability to combat some of the worst refugee crises in modern history. There are over 65.6 million forcibly displaced people, 22.5 million refugees and 10 million stateless people, whereas only 189,300 refugees were resettled in 2016. Continued volatile instability in Syria, Afghanistan, and South Sudan and the rise of xenophobia and anti-immigrant and refugee sentiment globally accentuate an already dire situation.

Additionally important is the potential for change in governance at the IMF. As early as 2006, the International Monetary Fund increased the voting rights of China, South Korea, Mexico, and Turkey, in response to those nations' growing economic power (Indian Express

2006). This shift in voting rights away from the hegemony of western powers and Japan was minimal, and further changes have been limited. Voting rights are directly linked to the national investment, or quota, made in the organization. The United States remains the most powerful member, with almost three times the voting power (16.52%) of its closest peer, Japan (6.15%). Voting shares increase with quota shares, which guarantees the ongoing dominance of the IMF by richer nations. The ability of these nations to exert power over the IMF, and thus over international financial architecture, will continue to be stymied by the disproportionate voting power of developed nations and the veto power of the United States.

Policy Options

- Convoke a global conversation about new ways to diminish the economic power of rich nations and corporations. Measures abound that make it clear that an extractive neoliberal economic policy can have only polarizing effects that increase the ranks of the poor while devastating the environment. Yet global governance organizations have not proved themselves able to hold such a conversation. This conversation must be led by organizations that are less captive to wealthy interests. The UN Millennium Development Goals could provide a model, but poor nations' voices need to be prioritized over those of rich nations.
- Organizations that might convoke such a conversation include the International Labour Organization, the New Economy Coalition, and Eurodad.
- Change voting structures at the UN to more accurately reflect democratic representation.
- Change voting structures at the IMF to reflect national need, rather than national power. To overturn the hegemony of neoliberal policy, the poor must have more powerful and guaranteed voices in institutions of power.
- Make sure all global economic and development decisions made by global bodies are vetted by global environmental consultants, the likes of which could be drawn from the Intergovernmental Panel on Climate Change.
- Impose taxes on speculation, such as the proposed Tobin Tax on "hot" money, which can fly across borders with the click of a computer mouse, in order to provide greater stability to national

economies, a fiscal base for development spending, and a retreat from speculation as a source of easy profits.

- Incorporate labor and environmental provisions in WTO trade negotiations that can be enforced without threat of "retaliation" due to perceivably unfair advantages.

Resources

Applebaum, R.P. and Lichtenstein, N. (2016) *Achieving Workers Rights in the Global Economy*, Ithaca, NY: Cornell University Press.

Gygli, S., Haelg, F. and Sturm, J.E. (2018) *The KOF Globalisation Index—Revisited*, KOF Working Paper, No. 439.

Intergovernmental Panel on Climate Change (2016) Climate Change 2014 Synthesis Report Summary for Policymakers. http://ipcc.ch/pdf/assessment-report/ar5/syr/AR5_SYR_FINAL_SPM.pdf

Luce, S. (2014) *Labor Movements Global Perspectives*, Malden, MA: Polity.

OECD (2015) Climate Change Mitigation: Policies and Progress. http://www.keepeek.com/Digital-Asset-Management/oecd/environment/climate-change-mitigation_9789264238787-en#.WnnXHoXf7sk#page2

Standing, G. (2017) *Basic Income: A Guide for the Open-Minded*, New Haven, CT: Yale University Press.

Swider, S. (2015) *Building China: Informal Work and the New Precariat*, Ithaca, NY: Cornell University Press.

United Nations Economic and Social Affairs (2016) *World Economic and Social Survey. Climate Change Resilience: An Opportunity for Reducing Inequalities*, United Nations: New York.

United Nations Environment Programme (2016) Rate of Environmental Damage Increasing Across Planet but Still Time to Reverse Worst Impacts, http://www.un.org/sustainabledevelopment/blog/2016/05/rate-of-environmental-damage-increasing-across-planet-but-still-time-to-reverse-worst-impacts/

World Trade Organization (n.d.) Nairobi Package, https://www.wto.org/english/thewto_e/minist_e/mc10_e/nairobipackage_e.htm

AFTERWORD

Looking Backwards to Move Everyone Forward to a More Inclusive, Just, and Sustainable World

Brian V. Klocke

The Society for the Study of Social Problems inaugurated the first *Agenda for Social Justice (Agenda)* in 2004, with the vision of presenting sociologically informed solutions for persistent social problems, to policy makers and the general public. While this fifth version of the *Agenda* is the first to emphasize global social problems, global issues and global actions for social justice have been a growing part of each *Agenda* publication.

The 2004 *Agenda* was written during a period which saw many contentious, large-scale global justice demonstrations at meetings of the World Trade Organization, the International Monetary Fund, the World Bank, and other gatherings, in primarily wealthy nations, that were expanding neoliberalism to benefit wealthy countries, corporations, and individuals at the detriment of the poor and the planet. Dr. Jon Shefner reminded readers of the first *Agenda*, in a chapter on global economics and protest, that "Legislation to improve civil rights, labor rights, and widen political participation all had antecedents in citizen protest."

In addition to protests against neoliberalism during the first decade of the 21st century, the World Social Forum (Forum) was expanding support, at its own annual meetings, for an alternative vision of a globalized world. The Forum sponsored open discussions and debates about solutions—enshrined in its founding Charter of Principles— to "the problems of exclusion and social inequality that the process of capitalist globalization with its racist, sexist and environmentally destructive dimensions is creating internationally and within countries."

The first section of the 2008 *Agenda* was titled "Global Issues" and featured a four-chapter section addressing the vulnerabilities of immigrant children, migrant workers, and low-income communities to global injustices and climate change disasters. An additional chapter addressed the opening for global policies advancing social justice in Latin America, due to what some scholars called the "pink tide" of citizens electing more liberal or leftist governments.

Our 2012 *Agenda* included chapters about the challenges of immigrant women and the need for immigration reform. By the time of its August publication, Latin America's pink tide began to recede to more conservative leaders that were less interested in challenging the orthodoxy of neoliberal globalization, and more interested in rolling back social programs addressing inequalities, as well as increasing authoritarian control. Part of the challenge of institutionalizing social change is getting governments to continue to work with social movements and marginalized groups to drive further policies to alleviate inequalities. Particular challenges of, but not exclusive to, many Latin American governments were overreliance on natural resource exploitation to fund progressive programs, and the difficulties of dealing with the remnants and continued pressures of operating within a neoliberal global economy.

The global optimism that ballooned in many countries upon the election of U.S. President Obama in 2008, seemed to have deflated by 2012, as the 2010 Arab Spring uprisings were violently suppressed and the 2011 Occupy Wall Street movement encampments, inspired by the Arab Spring, were destroyed. Obama's expansion of the military drone program, the failure to close Guantanamo prison, and increasing U.S. and global economic inequality, sucked even more air out of the balloon of hope for disadvantaged communities and countries devastated by war, climate crises, and food or water insecurity. All of these global problems were exacerbated by increasing commodification and financial speculation of extraction industries, consumer products, medicines, and food production, under global corporate capitalism. In the 2012 Afterword, I remarked about what I perceived to be a growing anger at bipartisan politics and frustration with the failed immigration, health care, and housing policies, plus institutionalized racism and sexism intertwined with increasing economic disparities. These comments foreshadowed disaffected voters' impact on the 2016 U.S. Presidential elections. This was clearer by the 2016 publication of our *Agenda*, when I described the left–right divide of the "anti-establishment" campaigns of Bernie Sanders and Donald Trump that had gained much support by spring. Our *Agenda* again had chapters suggesting elements of more informed social policies related to immigration and global labor issues, and an Afterword which explained that:

Social justice-based policy solutions require a shift in the dynamics of power that have created the social problems being addressed. Thus, the people that policies and programs are meant to serve must be included in the leadership directing the design and implementation of them, as well as provided access to resources to make it happen, without cooptation to the agendas of privileged groups, if the solutions are to be systemically effective and sustainable.

Since the first *Agenda* in 2004, authors and editors have realized that the social problems inherent in U.S. society and institutions impact global social problems in several ways, of which I will only briefly describe a few. As the dominant economic and military power of the world, with a long history of extensive direct and indirect intervention in the politics, policies, and armed conflicts of countries on every continent, the U.S. has had a strong hand in creating and influencing inequalities within and between countries. Secondly, the U.S. has disproportionate formalized power in global governance institutions, such as the U.N. Security Council, in which it has veto power, and the International Monetary Fund, where it has about three times the voting power of its closest peer, as Shefner and Christian explained in the previous chapter. Thirdly, while China is the largest emitter of CO_2—the primary contributor to global climate disruption—the U.S. is the second-largest, but has more than double the emissions per capita.

For this edition of *Global Agenda for Social Justice*, we have more chapters and more international scholars and institutions represented than any previous version of the *Agenda*. There are many important contributions in this volume to a research-informed approach to alleviating global social problems. I am only able to summarize a few of them in general themes within this allotted space. As in previous editions, the criminalization of marginalized groups and violence against those precariously situated in the global economy and conflict zones, such as migrants, women and girls, racial and ethnic minorities, to name a few, are a common concern.

There is an acknowledgement in this volume that lack of policies regulating cultural and technological industries in the public interest, during this digital age, has significant negative impacts on how citizens are able to access, navigate, and assess information relevant to their lives. It also can create and deepen social and political divides, or, if effective policies are implemented, can create better informed publics necessary for social movements and democratic action.

Authors have addressed the urgency of environmental issues and the crucial goal of energy democracy for addressing the disproportionate impacts of climate change. The persistence of fossil fuel-based energy systems has created and exacerbated climate disruption and related social problems. One of the biggest threads throughout the solutions for global social justice, from the first edition of the *Agenda* in 2004 to this greatly expanded volume of 2018, is how research shows that economic insecurity and inequality exacerbated by neoliberalism, is intimately connected with a multitude of global social, economic, and environmental problems.

During the last 15 years of publishing the *Agenda*, we have seen waves of progress and of retrenchment in addressing issues of global inequality and injustice. Since 2016, as indicated by the President of the Society for the Study of Social Problems at the beginning of this publication, we have seen a disturbing global resurgence in xenophobic, nationalist politics, and undemocratic, authoritarian regimes, combined with increasing global economic inequality. The challenge for global justice advocates moving forward is to figure out how best to reach out to and inform broader, divided publics about our interconnected global fates and the necessity of systemic transformation of outdated, unsustainable, and undemocratic institutions. Action without knowledge is futile, but awareness without action is ignorant. Our solutions must focus on actions that utilize the insights of sociology, to know how to bring people together to learn from each other and to create a better world before it is too late for all of us.

Key Resources

Union of Concerned Scientists. n.d. Each Country's Share of CO2 Emissions.
https://www.ucsusa.org/global-warming/science-and-impacts/science/each-countrys-share-of-co2.html#.Wr1FyWbMyV4
World Social Forum. 2001. World Social Forum Charter of Principles. http://www.universidadepopular.org/site/media/documentos/WSF_-_charter_of_Principles.pdf